Praise for
The Art of Prayer

"I cannot commend *The Art of Prayer* too highly. Here at last is a book on prayer that transcends traditions. Timothy Jones has given us a book that is deep, yet accessible; serious, yet with wonderful flashes of humor and insight. This is a book for spiritual pygmies who long to be giants—in short, a book for all of us."
—LORD CAREY, the 103rd Archbishop of Canterbury

"I often shrink from books about prayer because they usually produce in me feelings of inadequacy. I was delighted to find Tim Jones to be a sympathetic, not intimidating, guide. He writes with humility, clarity, and practicality—exactly the qualities I want in a book on prayer."
—PHILIP YANCEY, author of *Soul Survivor*

"[A] fine introduction to prayer as well as a deeply reflective meditation.... [This book] will appeal to a broad readership because of Jones's luminous prose and his lucid insights."
—*Publishers Weekly*

"Prayer, the expression of our deepest and most essential selves, also names our most pervasive inadequacy. And so we need guides, men and women who return us to our true selves and encourage us to do what is most natural to us. Timothy Jones is a reassuring guide: He guides us into a life of prayer not by cramming us with knowledge and technique but by quietly returning us to simplicity of soul and the presence of God."
—EUGENE PETERSON, translator of *The Message*

"A wisely human, spiritually practical, and wonderfully interesting book about the most important project of my life: deeper friendship and more effective communication with the Maker of the Universe.

If it proves half as helpful to others as it has already been to me, it will have been a splendid gift to us all."

— THE LATE LEWIS SMEDES, author of *Forgive and Forget*

"Many Americans, surveys reveal, are eager to have an encounter with the living God, yet they too often feel sidetracked by concern over such questions as Is God really approachable? and What do I say when I pray? Tim Jones addresses such concerns with clarity and freshness, enabling readers to come closer to realizing their heartfelt desire to hear and serve God."

— GEORGE GALLUP JR.

"Jones provides reassurance and inspiration on a topic of importance to a growing number of readers."

— *Library Journal*

THE
ART OF PRAYER

A

SIMPLE GUIDE TO

CONVERSATION WITH GOD

THE
ART OF PRAYER

TIMOTHY JONES

WATERBROOK
PRESS

THE ART OF PRAYER
PUBLISHED BY WATERBROOK PRESS
2375 Telstar Drive, Suite 160
Colorado Springs, Colorado 80920
A division of Random House, Inc.

Details in some anecdotes and stories have been changed to protect the identities of the persons involved.

ISBN 1-57856-849-8

An earlier edition of *The Art of Prayer* was published by Ballantine Books, copyright © 1997.

An earlier version of A Study Guide on Prayer in the appendix was originally published as a Fisherman Bible Studyguide titled *Prayer: Discovering What Scripture Says,* copyright © 1993 by Timothy Jones and Jill Zook-Jones.

Library of Congress Cataloging-in-Publication Data
Jones, Timothy K., 1955–
    The art of prayer : a simple guide to conversation with God / by Timothy Jones.—1st Water-Brook Press ed.
        p. cm.
    Originally published: New York : Ballantine Books, 1997.
    Includes bibliographical references.
    ISBN 1-57856-849-8
    1. Prayer—Christianity. I. Title.
BV215.J67 2005
248.3'2—dc22   2004027715

Printed in the United States of America
2005—First WaterBrook Press Edition

10 9 8 7 6 5 4 3 2 1

To Abram and Sarah,
with prayers for your new life together

CONTENTS

In every ordinary life there are the treadmills, the nitty-gritty routines that, though dull, are necessary for life, health, and well-being; and alongside them are set the wellsprings, the meat-and-drink activities that we celebrate as lifegiving, and in which, whatever problems and hurdles they may raise for us as we go along, we find unending pleasure, satisfaction, and contentment. It is as we keep returning to these wellsprings—the writer to his composing, the angler to his fishing, the organist to his keyboard, the gardener to his good earth, and so on—that we find ourselves assured of the essential richness of life and are moved to echo, with regard to these things, the words that Jelly Roll Morton sang long ago of "Doctor Jazz": "The more I have, the more I want, it seems." Many people in and around the churches, both those who labor to pray regularly and those who don't, would put praying in the first of these two categories, that of the routine. Timothy Jones wants us all to discover that in fact it belongs in the second. Most definitely—let me come clean—I want that too. Hence these paragraphs.

The Puritans of history, whose teaching about prayer was profound and is far less well known than it should be, made much of the fact that Christians, the sinners for whom Christ died and who are now justified through faith, are also adopted into God's family; and they stressed over and over that prayer is at heart children's conversation with their heavenly Father. Said Philip Henry, who sired Matthew Henry the commentator: "God regards not elegancy in prayer. He cares not how little there is of head in the duty, so there be a great deal of the *heart*.... We must approach God in prayer as children to a father.... Is not a tender-hearted father far more delighted with the lispings and stammerings of his little child, when it first begins to speak, than with the neatest, finest speech he can hear from another? And what is the reason? Why, it is *his child.*"[1] Grasping or, it would be better to say, being grasped by the truth of Henry's words is the watershed event that opens the door to real prayer. Boldness of access, confidence in God's open ear, trust in the reality of his love and care, and freedom to tell him things just the way we feel them, all flow directly from knowing that we belong to God's family, where the Lord Jesus Christ, our enthroned Savior and Sustainer, is our elder brother, and his and the Father's glory are what the family must constantly try to advance, and we are to cherish the promised prospect that we shall spend eternity glorified with Jesus and sharing his company and his joy.

It has often and, I think, truly and wisely been said that the best prayer in the world, the cry to God that best catches the spirit of the Psalms and the Lord's Prayer, is the one word "Help!" Without the sense of need and weakness, words addressed to God would not be prayer at all. Speaking of prayer as an art, therefore, might be risky; it might make us think of praying as a more studied and less spontaneous activity, more of an acquired technique of performance and less the opening of an anxious and often frazzled heart, than in fact it is.

Yet all that Timothy Jones says about right attitudes of mind being basic to meaningful prayer is vitally important. We do need to have some idea of the place of our praying in God's plan for our spiritual growth in Christ. We do need to remember that praying involves sometimes being quiet as well as persistently being verbal; sometimes listening to God, both as we read and meditate on his Word and as we hold up before him our present perplexities; sometimes deliberately stopping what we were saying about our troubles, tangles, and terrors in order to find again the peace that comes from realizing that he is almighty and loves us. We do need to let our Lord move us forward in the way we pray, so that we do not simply mark time, for our living is a journey, and one cannot take a journey by standing still. We do need to learn that when we have asked for help and strength to act, we should then go into action expecting to receive what we asked for.

The real art of praying is taking seriously the goodness and faithfulness of our heavenly Father, so that our life of prayer becomes part of the longer reality of our life of faith.

Timothy Jones knows what he is talking about as he writes of these things, and from the user-friendly beginner's book, all thoughtful Christians, wherever they are located on the path of prayer, will find that they learn a lot. So over now to you.

—J. I. PACKER
Regent College
Vancouver B.C.

ACKNOWLEDGMENTS

In the writing of this book, I received scores of insights from people through informal conversations, interviews, correspondence, even Internet postings. Their struggles, experiences, and discoveries have enriched this book wonderfully. Although most of these friends go unnamed, their comments appear throughout this book, and I am grateful.

I also thank those who read and offered comments on early drafts, including Kevin Miller, Peter Shockey, Ken Abraham, and especially my wife, Jill Zook-Jones. My heartfelt thanks also to my editor, Elisa Fryling Stanford, for her wise and skillful editing, and to the entire WaterBrook team.

Introduction

FIRST STEPS

At the profoundest depths of life, people talk not
about God but with him.

—D. ELTON TRUEBLOOD

My soul thirsts for you.

—KING DAVID OF ISRAEL, Psalm 63:1

Sometimes I find myself astonished by how interested people
seem in spiritual things. Prayer is capturing our imaginations
like never before. A major newsweekly reported several years ago that
more Americans prayed than exercised, went to work, or had sex.[1] Talk
to executive or mechanic, college student or retiree, churchgoer or
skeptic, and you find phenomenal spiritual fascination. When asked
in a national poll, "Do you experience in your life a need for spiritual
growth?" eight out of ten Americans said yes.

I think of my sister-in-law in New Jersey. She has little interest in
church and traditional faith, yet she finds herself longing to pray. She
finds herself drawn to spiritual matters. "Sometimes when I see something beautiful—a baby laughing, the sun coming up—I feel moved
to give a short prayer of thanks." Wonderful moments tug at something deep within her.

Hard things also make us aware of our spiritual hunger. Hearing
an ominous report from a medical test, grieving from a divorce, seeing

our children riding bumpily through adolescence—such moments drive us to pour out our souls to someone beyond ourselves. Ellen Gulden, the main character in the contemporary novel *One True Thing*, watched her cancer-ridden mother receive chemotherapy "drop by drop by please-let-it-work-God drop." What did she do?

> Oh yes, I prayed in that [hospital] cubicle and in the hallway
> outside and in the cafeteria, where I went as much to shake
> the feeling of being buried alive…as much as because I really
> wanted another cup of coffee. But I prayed to myself without
> form, only inchoate feelings, one word: please, please, please,
> please.[2]

As I look back over my forty-plus years of life, I realize how often such experiences have prompted me to pray, how life's crises and little anxieties and quiet joys make me long for satisfying prayer. A friend of mine calls it our ache for cosmic specialness. No longer will mere belief in something "out there" do. We want to talk to God. We want to relate to God. "You have made us for yourself," prayed Augustine centuries ago, "and our heart is restless until it rests in you."[3] Something tells us he was right. Sometimes prayer seems like the most natural response to life you can imagine.

But for all of our inclination to pray, many of us are still searching for *how*. Or if we have some know-how, we still sense that we're missing something. Other people's experiences with God somehow seem more fulfilling than our own. Sometimes our prayers seem no more satisfying than Ellen Gulden's blurted, barely formed feelings.

Most of us want to find a way of praying that gives our lives richness and hope. When we talk to God, can we do better than stutter? Can we move beyond stale habit? Is it possible to pray with confidence? Can time spent with God really transform us? We sense that prayer can be more than a rote response to an admonition, maybe even something exciting. But how? Anne Lamott tells of a friend whose prayer each morning consists of "Whatever." And whose prayer at the end of day is "Oh, well."[4] I laughed when I read that, but I also asked, "Can't there be more?"

❖

When I was growing up in Southern California, living through the momentous decades of the sixties and seventies, my family "said grace" at meals. I was vaguely aware that my parents prayed at other times, away from the dinner table. My father once told me in hushed tones about a moving experience he had had on a New England hillside: As a young man he was overtaken by a dawning, amazing awareness of God's presence. I don't remember many details; perhaps he supplied few to start with. Were he alive, I would ask him more. But I knew then that he had experienced something powerful, and he said he was never the same afterward.

My mother, too, sometimes mentioned spiritual matters—how prayer and her rural Tennessee Methodist roots kept her going through a miscarriage, through colon cancer, through everyday life. "How do people who don't believe in God or pray get through hard times?" she would sometimes ask, rhetorically more than anything else.

And every week Sunday school and church were part of our family's routine. Prayer formed a kind of backdrop in our house, an almost invisible assumption, and I learned much from my parents' example. But we almost never talked about prayer and even less often talked about how to *do* it.

I went on to major in religious studies in college and then to complete a master's degree in pastoral studies at a prestigious theological school. But even there I was largely on my own when it came to the actual encounter of my soul with God. Apart from some notable exceptions—a pastor here, a professor there—few people offered consistent spiritual guidance. I felt strongly attracted to prayer, but I questioned and struggled.

My questions and explorations continue. I have seen enough of life to vouch for the words of David Jeremiah, who writes, "I have found that prayer is the most wonderful gift in God's great bag of blessings."[5] Yet I still long to experience that moving encounter more deeply. But how?

❖

If you are like me, if you feel ready to go further and deeper into the experience of prayer, several questions or concerns may greet you when you decide to move from mere attraction to actual practice. As I have looked back on my own praying, talked to scores of friends, and ransacked countless books, I have found that the following questions make many of us hesitate.

Is God really approachable? Like Dorothy and her ragamuffin band on their way to Oz, we may need to find courage to draw near to God. We may not expect the billowing smoke and booming voice that Dorothy encountered when she approached the wizard, but we may feel unworthy or afraid, and our fears drive a wedge between us and whatever picture we have of God. Time after time I have heard people say they do not feel "good enough" to pray—even people who have prayed and attended church for years. They are convinced God won't greet them kindly, let alone love them. For many of us, a particular sin, a lifetime of spiritual apathy, the fear we haven't "measured up," even the feeling that we haven't prayed enough may leave us thinking that God is holding himself at arm's distance. We need to know, Will God greet me when I come to him? It's hard for us to believe the words of Wesley Duewel: "The greatest privilege God gives you is the freedom to approach Him any time. You are not only authorized to speak to Him; you are invited. You are not only permitted; you are expected. God waits for you to communicate with Him."[6] But wouldn't we love to be convinced this is true?

Does God care enough to listen when we speak? "For so many years," a woman confessed to her counselor and spiritual mentor, "there had been a high, impenetrable wall between God and myself. I used to throw my little gifts over the wall and hope that someone was on the other side receiving them. It was impersonal, unsatisfying, but I thought it was the best I could do or even hope for."[7] We tell ourselves that we should pray more often and that we would if we knew for sure God was listening. For our prayer to seem real, God needs to be a vivid, personal Presence. So we wonder how to grow such a conviction.

What do I say when I pray? How do I find the actual words? Are there certain words or phrases we need to use in prayer to get it "right"? Vaguely remembered lines from church or other religious settings help us some. Maybe we have mimicked others or experimented enough to have fashioned a makeshift formula for praying. A friend of mine, admitting his feelings of inadequacy in prayer, once confessed, "I try to use big-sounding theological words when I pray because I'm afraid God won't hear me otherwise." Prayer sometimes seems like an enterprise reserved for mystics, for those whose schedules allow them to trek to mountaintop retreats or master the catch phrases of the religious professionals. How do we find satisfying prayer times?

I used to feel closer to God. Can I get it back? If you were raised in a practicing, faithful household, you may not experience a lack of words or belief as much as a cooling of spiritual passion. You don't doubt the great tenets of faith and devotion as much as you sense that your soul needs reviving. You feel spiritually numb. You'd like to see your faith thaw, warm, and perhaps even catch fire. As hurried and harried as your schedule is, you realize that nothing less than heartfelt faith will keep you going in the practice of prayer. Yet you sometimes wonder: Is my desire genuine? Do I really *want* to make room for a growing relationship with God, especially when I think about the changes it may demand?

Will God actually respond to my prayers? We hear stories of people who claim that God got them or a loved one out of a jam because they prayed. Philip Yancey tells of growing up in a church so filled with expectancy that the atmosphere on Sunday mornings was, as he says, "humid with miracles."[8] People would tell of answered prayers in the finding of a lost fountain pen or the opening up of parking spaces when women took their children to the doctor. But the anecdotes do not always jibe with our daily experiences, or at least our feelings. Will we see such results when we pray? We have all sincerely, desperately pleaded for release from a prison of pain or illness or for some hoped-for promotion or reprieve, only to experience disappointment with God. What if God seems to turn to us a deaf ear? Do we dare risk praying if we might not get the answer we expect?

I believe that the answers to such questions about prayer are ultimately quite simple. That is where this book can help. Our not knowing exactly how prayer works need not keep us from its delights. The fact that we fumble for words does not disqualify us. Prayer is for nonexperts. It is possible—and important—for the person with the slightest stirring of spiritual interest to begin to pray. I believe that prayer can be wonderfully uncomplicated. Indeed, the working title for this book was *Prayer Made Simple.*

A book on prayer, I should also underscore, is not like a book on chemistry or carpentry. Talking to God is more art than science. It does not require technique as much as relationship. It has more to do with will than skill. Conversation with God involves our deepest selves and our most everyday moments.

So while plumbing the depths of prayer can take a lifetime, and while prayer is not always *easy,* it can be as unpretentious and unadorned as talking to a caring friend. At its barest definition, prayer is simply the language of relationship between us and God.

A forty-something woman who had wandered for years amid a salad bar of spiritualities once wrote me, "I have a feeling my prayer life is shifting into high gear these days. I'm learning how to talk to God again in plain old words."

When we pray, then, we can use simple words from the heart. "In the morning, O LORD," penned a psalm writer centuries ago, "you hear my voice; in the morning I lay my requests before you and wait in expectation" (Psalm 5:3). That verse represents both a prayer and a clue to how simple prayer sometimes is. While we will realize again and again how much room for growth in intimacy with God lies ahead, the present moment, with all its possibilities and problems, always provides the most promising starting place.

⁘⬥⬥⬥⬥⬥⬥⁘

I once heard someone use an expression that helped me better understand what the art of prayer may look like. It's a phrase I've used myself, in fact, but hearing him say it made me realize how odd it sounds. He was talking about being "hungry" for God. Hunger has a very earthy side—a rumbling stomach, an impulse to chew, a desire to be satisfied. It may not seem at first a promising image for such a lofty topic as the spiritual life. But my friend was on to something. When we do not eat, gnawing appetite drives us to the refrigerator. And when we neglect our soul hunger or fill it with spiritual junk food, we know we need something more. That hunger tells us something. And it is a cause for hope.

For our hunger was placed in us by One who knows best how to satisfy it. "I know," wrote Henri Nouwen, "that the fact that I am always searching for God, always struggling to discover the fullness of Love, always yearning for complete truth, tells me that I have already been given a taste of God, of Love and of Truth."⁹ That we want to pray suggests we can. That we pine to pray so powerfully and persistently suggests that Someone is waiting for us to speak, waiting to listen.

Fortunately, we need no mysterious etiquette to open up the rich joys of prayer. The desire to pray itself is all we need to start. "We approach God through love, not navigation," Augustine once wrote.

Not through charts and lists and abstractions, but with a simple, willing heart. In our seeking we can be found. In our reaching out we will be met.

Prayer, then, begins with whoever I am, wherever I may be, whatever I can give. You are ready to begin praying the moment you sense that there is something more to life and to faith than you now know. You won't want to—and don't need to—stop there. But such talking to God, simple and stuttering as it may be, can lead to a relationship far beyond what you may have ever thought possible. This book can help make that possibility a reality.

PRAYERS

Help us, Lord, to turn toward you, and in our turning, find that you have been turned toward us all along. Amen.

⋅⊱═◉═⊰⋅

Lord, you stir [us] to take pleasure in praising you, because you have made us for yourself, and our heart is restless until it rests in you.

—AUGUSTINE, *Confessions*

⋅⊱═◉═⊰⋅

Father in heaven, when the thought of you wakes in our hearts, let it not wake like a frightened bird that flies about in dismay, but like a child waking from its sleep with a heavenly smile.

—SØREN KIERKEGAARD

PART I

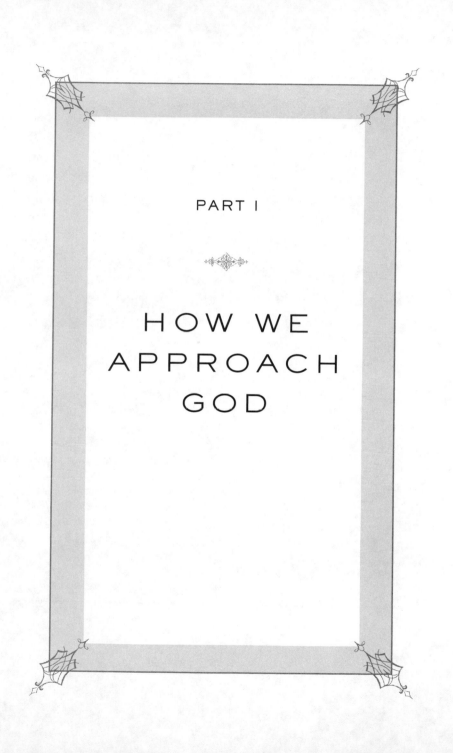

HOW WE APPROACH GOD

A Cry for Help

It does not need to be a formal prayer: the most stumbling and broken cry—a sigh, a whisper, anything that tells the heart's loneliness and need and penitence—can find its way to him.

—Phillips Brooks

I have been driven many times to my knees by the overwhelming conviction that I had nowhere else to go. My own wisdom, and that of all about me, seemed insufficient for the day.

—Abraham Lincoln

Never will I forget the terror of one night several years ago. My wife and family and I were living in a second-story apartment in a suburb in the Midwest. It would have been a typical bedtime, except my sons couldn't seem to get settled. As they jumped out of their bunk bed to use the bathroom one more time, the thudding sound of their small feet on the floor infuriated our downstairs neighbor, whose bedroom, we suppose, was directly below theirs. He flew into a rage, ran up the stairs in our building, and began pounding on our door.

"Open this door," he screamed, "or I'll kill you!"

With images of a fist (or worse) in my face, I refused. He ran back down the steps and out into the parking lot, where he stood below our window, yelling and bellowing his threats.

With shaky hands, I dialed 911 for help. But just as intently and instinctively, I prayed. I don't recall what I said, but my words surely made up in urgency what they lacked in eloquence. By the time the police came and settled our neighbor down, we had already gathered as a family to pray aloud. Through trembling words, the kids uttered prayers beautiful in directness and simplicity: "Keep us safe. Help us!"

Need often prompts me to turn to God; many of my prayers over the years have arisen in similarly needy times. Waiting for word on a job I have longed for, smarting in the wake of a friend's snub, worrying about a doctor's frown over my wife's medical test—such moments make me eager to find resources beyond my own. More than once, worries about a project at work have kept me awake in the wee hours. As I lay in bed those dark mornings, I have found in my worry great energy and motivation to pray. Time and again, the things that stress and trouble me have made me a praying man, a more spiritually open person.

But occasionally I wonder, *Shouldn't prayer have to do with loftier things?* I notice how often my praying chronically grows out of daily concerns—my vocation and work, our family budget, my children's health. Does God mind if I come to him with my anxieties and everyday misfortunes? "I've been committed to God for twenty years," a close friend once admitted, "and have long heard the idea that I should always begin my praying with thankfulness and adoration of God. But try as I might to do differently, I enter prayer with things that burden me."

The idea of coming to God with our everyday burdens makes many of us uncomfortable. Some people are so uneasy that they conclude that prayer prompted by need belongs to preschool piety. We "outgrow" the impulse to come to God for "favors" or help, I have heard them say. People even make fun of such praying, lumping it with the sentiment of the Janis Joplin song that asks God to buy her a Mercedes-Benz because her friends all drive Porsches. Only the self-ish or spiritually immature will turn to God in need, we hear. So we hesitate to come to God with what bothers us.

⊰⊰⟡⊱⊱

Years of praying have convinced me of the validity of prayers born of desperation. My needy moments drive me to prayer, and I believe God is happy to have me come to him. Not that I want such cries for help to be the only form of prayer I turn to; still, none of us coasts through life without sometimes needing help. Who of us has smarts and stamina and insight enough to always get us by? So we often must look outside ourselves. And at precisely those moments, we may be spiritually open as never before. We let our needs drive us to God.

As we do, we will discover several realities about prayer.

Prayer Begins Where We Are, Not Where We Think We Should Be

Perhaps no other conviction has done more to free me to turn to God. I come "just as I am," as an old gospel hymn has it. How could any of us pray otherwise? "Pray as you can, not as you can't," said one wise spiritual teacher.[1] If that means my prayers are earthy or needy, so be it. If I come somewhat desperately, God understands.

Many of the prayers I read in the Bible are rough-edged and unre-fined to an astonishing degree, even to the point of asking God to unleash vengeance on an enemy. They sometimes make me wince. But seeing such raw intensity reminds me that I can blurt out my words in panic or pain, not just when I am feeling holy. God wants *me*. I do not put on airs or try to give myself a spiritual makeover to talk to God. I turn my worries into cries for help. I let my fears nudge me to God. I let my need become a kind of energy for spiritual movement.

Brother Giles, one of the earliest followers of Francis of Assisi in the twelfth century, once told of a shy peasant woman whose only son had been arrested for a crime. As the young man was being led away to be hanged, Giles asked,

> Would not that woman, although shy and simple, scream, with disheveled hair and bared breast, and run to ask the king to free her son? Who—I ask you—taught that simple woman to make a petition for her son? Did not necessity and her love for her son make that shy woman (who previously hardly went beyond the threshold of her house) almost daring, running and screaming through the streets among men? And did it not make a simple person wise? Just so he who truly knew his own evils, dangers, and losses would be able to pray well—and would want to do so.[2]

As with that woman, our reaching out in need may make our praying real. Our praying will finally go beyond polite formalities. We might finally get honest about what makes us tick, or who ticks us off. It will be the authentic "I" who speaks.

The need that drives us to prayer, I find, is not just desperate need, not just the alarm of crisis. Boring sameness and mind-numbing normality become for many of us slower, more deliberate emergencies. Such flat stretches in life, when not much exciting seems to be happening, when we give up hope for change, can turn us outside ourselves. The restlessness they leave in us can move us to turn to God. Which leads to a second reality about prayer.

Prayer Thrives in the Soil of Daily Realities, Not Just in the Stratosphere of Devotion

We live lives of little things, I once heard someone say. Because God cares about the details, because he knows that daily commutes and dirty diapers and mortgage payments and drawn-out divorces consume our waking hours, our conversation with God can and should embrace these things. "Anything large enough for a wish to light upon," said George MacDonald, "is large enough to hang a prayer on."[3]

So I try to pray in a way that does not cut me off from the concrete dailyness of my life. I live at an intersection of particulars and details I cannot seem to ignore. No wonder I so much like the title of a spiritual classic by Jean-Pierre de Caussade, *The Sacrament of the Present Moment*. We find traces of the sacred in the corners of the everyday, even in the bland and repetitious. Where we live and *are* is where we pray. Why try to begin at any other place?

But perhaps you wonder, *Does a big God really care about my daily particulars?* After all, "God is in heaven and you are on earth," goes the proverb in Ecclesiastes 5:2, "so let your words be few." God's thoughts soar above ours. "As the heavens are higher than the earth, so are my ways higher than your ways," God says through the prophet in Isaiah 55:9. But while God inhabits realms far beyond our comprehension, I like to remember that he stands as close as our breath. Jesus reminded us that God numbers the hairs on our heads. (Although I notice a steadily receding hairline, many, many fine strands of hair still cover my scalp.) Even this amazing complexity, Jesus tells us, God somehow keeps track of. I have to conclude, then, that God is relentlessly, extravagantly concerned about the puny details of our lives. What if, rather than frowning on our needy requests, he delights in answering them with corresponding concreteness? What if he does not despise our urgent coming or even hesitate to notice and know us?

I recall a difficult day I had some time ago. I was leading a marathon board meeting at the publishing company where I was working at the time. Deadlines had left me scrambling at the last second to pull together the meeting's agenda. I felt flustered going into the meeting. To top it off, I had somehow managed to arrive without my own copy of a proposal I needed to lead a discussion. While I was very publicly reaching across the conference table to borrow a copy from a colleague, I knocked over a cup, spilling coffee and making a mess.

Even now, that clumsy moment captures and symbolizes a day I would rather forget.

The next morning, as I sat in my living room praying, I opened to the Psalms. My eyes fell on Psalm 20: "May the LORD answer you when you are in distress; may the...God of Jacob protect you.... May he give you the desire of your heart and make all your plans succeed" (verses 1,4). I began praying that God would show tender care to my bruised ego.

I felt no great ecstasies, but prayer suddenly became keenly relevant. My performance at a committee meeting may not seem like much when wars are looming or people are dying of AIDS, but every corner and crevice of our lives—even the gritty, sometimes-not-so-pleasant details—provide material for prayer.

Surely, then, the material of life matters: Kissing my wife good-bye in the morning, standing at the sink washing dishes, spending time with a parishioner who has lost a loved one, sitting at my desk trying to concentrate on my writing—there is no event or situation so commonplace that God cannot be invited in. I can bring these and a thousand other grains from my life into my conversation with God.

Prayer for Daily Matters Teaches Us That We Live Not by Ourselves but in Dependence on God

Prayers borne of need not only come naturally, they also teach us something profound about our relationship to God. Some of the holiest, most whole people I know realize that they are not the captains of their souls. They know their expertise is not sufficient for all that life brings. For many of them that lesson came when a business venture came crashing down, a longed-for baby miscarried, a father died. They came to the place of saying, "I need a power inside me that comes from beyond me."

Prayer borne of need can teach us that kind of humble dependence. I wonder if God may even allow us to meet times of profound need because he knows that they have potential to turn us toward him. Not that he inflicts pain, but he knows how in difficult times we are less likely to believe the myth that our ingenuity and self-sufficiency are adequate.

Such moments can also bring us profound insights about God's care. When need drives us beyond ourselves, we discover a gracious, kind God who waits to bless us. "Come to me, all you who are weary and burdened," is the invitation, "and I will give you rest" (Matthew 11:28). Our resources may not be adequate, but God's are. We can take our need to God and leave it in his hands.

Prayer That Begins in Need
Often Grows into Something Deeper

The anxiety that prompts us to turn to God may quiet once we are in his presence. As we, in prayer, meet a God of inexhaustible resources, our desperation may relax a bit. We may find ourselves free to think about something more than our own need. Prayer widens the horizons of our view, just as cresting a mountain road may break open before us a breathtaking vista.

So we pray like mad for a child going into surgery (and all the more if that child is *ours*). We pray to keep our job when it's threatened. We pray to pass an exam. But we also stay open, once we are in God's presence, to whatever he may do or show us.

A student named Michael Allen found this:

I remember when I was in [graduate school] my best friend accused me of some dark and desperate betrayal. I did not know what it was about. But I was angry. I was angry at this friend who had rejected me. And I went to the chapel to try to work it out. I knelt down and my prayer came out in a mass of feeling. I pleaded with God to avenge me, to destroy my friend. And I thought of all the ways the God of Israel, the Lord of the armies, who visits the sins of the father on the children, could do this thing. I savored my own anger,

and then it began to taste bad. And the anger began to sub-
side. Something else was welling up inside of me. And the
something else was hurt, my own desperate hurt that my
friend had rejected me, that I had lost someone I loved. And
then I wept and asked the Lord to give me back my friend.[4]

Such insight often becomes clear only when we sit in God's presence with our swirling feelings and poured-out cries. If we hold back,
fearing that we are not pure enough, we might never work through to
the other side. As Ann and Barry Ulanov write, "What we thought
was simply blind desire, starting out on its own, with nowhere in particular to go, turns out to be instead desire expressing a dim awareness
of something already there.... But we do not discover this if we
suppress or skip over our desires."[5] If God wants to take our needy
prayers and shape and transform them, he can. We can speak urgently
and let him temper our excesses if he thinks he should. But in the
meantime, we need not worry. We come, neediness and all.

⊷⊰◈⊱⊶

The fear I felt during my Friday-night encounter with my bellowing
neighbor—and my blurted prayers—turned out not to be the last
word.

That Sunday my family and I went to church. The pastor stood
up at the beginning of the service and said, somewhat apologetically,
"I don't normally do this, but I feel moved to say that this place is a
safe place. Some of you come from dangerous situations. But here you
are safe."

Pastor Lobs had no idea what had happened to us just two nights
before. He had no way of knowing about our jangled nerves and anxious thoughts. And he could not guess how much that word would
mean to a family still suffering the jitters.

Was it coincidence? I prefer to believe that God knew what we had just been through. He knew we needed him. Not only did God not mind our coming to him with our panicked prayers, he did us one better. He gave us a wonderfully timed word of encouragement. He met us in our need.

PRAYERS

Lord, I see that I am not enough in myself. I think I can go along without giving you a thought. But then I stumble. Or I grow afraid. Or someone pains me.

Then I remember you. Be close to me in my need. And help me to love you even when no worry knocks on my door. Amen.

⊷━◉═⊷

God our Father who urges us to pray, who makes it possible for us to pray, our plea is made to you, for when we pray to you we live better and we are better.

Hear me groping in these glooms, and stretch out your right hand to me. Shed your light on me, call me back from my wanderings. Bring yourself to me so that I may in the same way return to you.

—AUGUSTINE

THE SIMPLEST LANGUAGE

IN THE WORLD

To God we use the simplest, shortest words we can find
because eloquence is only air and noise to him.

—FREDERICK WILLIAM ROBERTSON

Your Father knows what you need before you ask him.

—JESUS, Matthew 6:8

Crying to God is not done with the physical voice, but
with the heart.... If, then, you cry to God, cry out
inwardly where he hears you.

—AUGUSTINE

When my youngest son was two years old, chronic ear infections
filled his ears with fluid, dulled his hearing, and slowed his
mastery of speech. Micah wanted to talk, but a lack of words constantly frustrated his attempts. This made his part in our family's
nightly bedside prayers a genuine trial for Micah, especially when he
took his turn after his highly verbal five-year-old brother, who managed, it seemed, to include in his prayers every neighbor and cousin
he ever knew.

But Micah so yearned to participate that he bowed his head and prayed in what can only be described as an unrolling string of word-like sounds and syllables. His praying had all the rhythm and inflection of real language. In the darkness of the boys' room, his solemn efforts left us all alternating between stifled laughter and awe.

Not long after witnessing Micah's often mumbled praying, our family moved to a suburb of Houston to gather a new congregation and build a new church. Sent off with the good wishes of friends and family, confident of our gifts and pastoral training, my wife and I went with high hopes. But almost as soon as we arrived, boomtown Houston went bust. The city's oil-industry economy dried up. People in our church moved away in search of jobs. After a year we realized that our fledgling venture was not going to meet expectations—not ours, not those of our financial backers. My wife and I slogged through two more years before we resigned, recommending that the church fold.

During that difficult time I would sometimes awaken in the mornings with a dull emotional ache. I prayed often; indeed, my prayer times became more frequent. But sometimes the best I could bring to my morning prayers was a groaning spirit. No elegant, high-flying prose. No eminently quotable lines. Just a heartfelt reaching out for comfort in words that, should anyone have overheard them, fell far short of articulate.

For all my adult facility with language, I am sometimes like Micah when I pray. So, perhaps, are you. Words do not always come easily for expressing the complex emotions that swirl within. Or in the presence of unfathomable majesty, we wonder, *What can I say?* Or we think, *If God is One, as an ancient prayer says, "from whom no secrets are hid" how can I help being intimidated?* "I want to pray," I hear people say, "but I'm afraid I won't find the right words." Like the terror a writer feels when faced with a blank page waiting to be filled with words, the prospect of addressing God can make us freeze up. We get "pray-er's block." Or we push on ahead, but it feels as if we are just going through the motions. "Sometimes," a friend once admitted to me, "I throw in big words just to make it all sound more 'theological.'" We stutter along. We worry so much about our words that our approach to God falters.

What can we do when words make us stumble?

❖

To begin with, I try to remember that words do not matter to God as much as many of us suppose. They carry less weight than we think.

Our culture seems infatuated by words. By the millions they stream from our radios, televisions, newspapers, Internet sites, and yes, books. Drive through any metropolitan area, with its billboards, neon ads, and bannered signs, and you get the strange sensation of driving through a phone book or huge dictionary.[1] Words seem essential. But much that is profound can happen in their absence.

"Your thoughts don't have words every day," wrote even the stunningly articulate Emily Dickinson.[2] And when it comes to prayer, our spiritual impulses don't always need words either. What lies deepest within us does not need dazzling utterance. We may pray most profoundly when we actually say little. "The best prayers," noted seventeenth-century writer John Bunyan, "often have more groans than words." For all their roughness, both Micah's praying and mine plumbed depths that polished phrases can never touch. Who knows how much Micah made up in sincerity what he lacked in fluency? And I remember my dark time in Texas as a time of growing depth and intimacy with God.

Stumbling over the words need not make any of us feel like second-class pray-ers. For in prayer, as in so many enterprises, we do well to make our words not the goal but the means. We aim not so much for eloquence (even though that may sometimes come) but for simplicity. When words cease being ends in themselves, we can relax with them. We stop being like the anxious teenager on his first date, trying so hard to be the witty conversationalist that his date can tell he's straining. Instead, we just talk with God. "We don't need to use

high-sounding words or try to structure our sentences to impress any-
body," one woman explained. "I like to think of the Lord as sitting in
a chair near me and I am conversing with Him."[3] This simple approach
can free us in prayer to focus on relationship, not form. Words become
a tool to use in our spiritual work, not the goal of the work. We
approach them as a wire or switch or other electrical conductor. We
realize they play a vital part in conveying what we long to express, but
they are not themselves the power that drives the motor or lights the
filament. Words do not by themselves make prayer "happen."

Rather than defining prayer as something solely expressed in
words, I see it more fundamentally as being present to God. Sometimes words are eminently appropriate. Sometimes they get in the
way. Often they simply don't matter. The important thing is to stand
before God without our constant chatter, ready to be in heartfelt relationship to him. Where our whole selves are engaged in relationship
with God, there prayer will be, even if words are not used.[4]

I also believe that our longing to pray in itself holds great promise for
getting us through our difficulty. Our wanting is a great ally. We move
ahead when we attend to our *desire* to pray. For the desire that propels
us is ultimately a quest for intimacy with God, for a relationship that
will go beyond words.

Our desire to express ourselves in the first place runs deep and
early in our makeup. Linguists (and any parent) will tell you that
babies seem to have an innate drive to talk. They don't need vocabulary drills and other formal training techniques in order to learn. They
begin to pick up words without prodding or pushing. The urge to talk,
like the urge to walk, seems built into our genes. A child *wants* to squall
out his or her need for milk or giggle with affectionate patter or call
out for Daddy. We so long to relate to others, to express what is within,
to hear what is within others, that language simply "happens."

While prayer sometimes seems difficult, it is also something we want to do. In one sense, then, nothing is more natural than praying; nothing arises more readily than turning our wants and moments of wonder into speech. Once I read that learning to pray is like mastering a foreign language. But that analogy breaks down. Yes, there are patterns we learn to follow, words we find from listening to others, but because we are made to relate to God, prayer is not foreign to our hearts. Spending time with God does not usually require herculean effort, if only we pay attention to our truest desires, placed there by a Creator who made us restless until we find our rest in him.

Psychiatrist Gerald May illustrates this with a story. Once he asked a young woman what she most deeply wanted. She responded immediately with typical concerns: a happy home and family, security, a sense of being worthwhile. Then May asked her to sit in silence for a moment and try to be open to what desires she could really *feel*. After a while, he said,

> She looked up with tears in her eyes.… "What I actually feel is that things are really okay right now. Better than okay. I don't think I want anything more than what I have at this very moment." I asked her to be still once again, to look more deeply into her present feeling, to seek any desire that might honestly be there. Softly, she said, "…I want to say thank you to someone. Is it God? If it is, I want to…say thanks."[5]

The urge to turn to God is part of who we are, if only we listen long enough.

This means that when we do pray, the most profound prayer is often the simplest because it arises from deep within, from some primal part of us from whence come not only words but also memories, hurts, hopes, and all that makes us who we are. You don't need to be an expert in theological vocabulary to speak to God. You do need to be yourself. Prayer is the simplest language in the world. Micah discovered that.

Indeed, the prayers of the great figures of the Bible display a disarming lack of complication. Moses stammered his way through the times he had to address the people of Israel. "O Lord," he complained, "I have never been eloquent, neither in the past nor since you have spoken to your servant. I am slow of speech and tongue" (Exodus 4:10). And yet, we read later that before God he conversed freely, "face to face" (Exodus 33:11). That picture of Moses shows us that prayer need not be eloquent to be real; it need only come from our true selves.

Prayer, then, may employ the most elementary speech, the most natural expression. "Often," said John Climacus, a sixth-century Byzantine church leader, "it is the simple, repetitious phrases of a little child that our Father in heaven finds most irresistible."

I am startled to hear spiritual giants, who could wax eloquent in prayer if anyone could, stress the same thing. The fourth-century monk Abba Macarius, for example, was asked, "How should one pray?" The elderly man said, "There is no need at all to make long discourses; it is enough to stretch out one's hand and say, 'Lord, as you will, and as you know, have mercy.' And if the conflict grows fiercer, say: 'Lord, help.' He knows very well what we need and shows us mercy."⁶ What could be simpler? "Help!" is prayer in fine form, jangled exclamation and all.

The nineteenth-century saint Thérèse of Lisieux wrote of the folly of feeling as though she needed some "formula of words" to pray: "I just do what children have to do before they learn to read. I tell God what I want quite simply, without any splendid turns of phrase, and somehow He always manages to understand me."⁷

This approach can free us to pray more naturally wherever we find ourselves. Some of my best praying, I suspect, is done off the cuff and on the run, literally. Sometimes I pray when I jog. I also pray when I drive to work, when I wait in line somewhere, when I drift off to sleep. Prayer at such times is possible because it can pour out unrehearsed and spontaneous. We can do "quick takes." We can cry out from the heart of our mundane or manic lives.

You do not need to be in a pulpit or sanctuary; you do not need to have a prayer book open in front of you. You do not need *thee*s and *thou*s. Although God is awe inspiring and almighty, prayer can still take on the qualities of daily conversation. You can converse with God as with a friend, with unselfconscious naturalness. What takes up room in your heart can appear in your prayers.

⋯⬦⬦⬦⋯

When words don't come, it helps me to remember another thing: God does not stand far off as I struggle to speak to him. He cares enough to listen with more than casual attention. He "translates" my scrubby words and hears what is truly inside. He hears my sighs and uncertain gropings as if they were fine prose. We do not like to stand speechless or stammering before God, but that does not mean God holds it against us when we do.

I remember a vacation with my parents in France when I was in high school. I had just completed two years of French, enough to learn the rudiments, but hardly enough to make me fluent. Still, there we were, tourists wanting to make the most of our time. So when we needed a bathroom, when we wanted to find a café, or when I lost my eyeglasses on the steps of L'Église du Sacré-Coeur and approached a police officer for help, I falteringly used my butchered French. I was trying—to the politely suppressed laughter of others—to speak the language. But I remember more than the townspeople's bemusement. I remember how they warmly received my efforts. They strained to hear past my fractured sentences and hopeless American accent. They honored me by responding. Is God any less generous?

According to a Jewish tradition, King David asked God to "understand what is in my heart."[8] Another Jewish tradition has it that God hears the faintest whisper.[9] "Before a word is on my tongue," said the psalmist, "you know it completely, O LORD" (139:4). That is a wonderful picture.

God hears all that arises from us—the words of our mouths, the longings of our hearts, the thoughts of our minds, the intentions of our wills. Regret, grief, thanksgiving, hope—God hears our emotions, not just our grammar. Because of his grace, not our eloquence, we can pray. Even if we stammer and stutter.

⁘⊰◈⊱⁘

I take heart in another reality of prayer: God helps me form even the words. He joins his own powerful presence to what I try to say and do. A Someone beyond my words comes and fills them out. "In the same way," wrote Paul the apostle, "the Spirit helps us in our weakness. We do not know what we ought to pray for, but the Spirit himself intercedes for us with groans that words cannot express" (Romans 8:26).

There were times during those trying days in Texas when emotional energy failed to well up in abundance. When my words were few and my spirit was tired, I had to depend on resources that went deeper than my own. So I would open my heart and my mind in the presence of God. I did not try hard to say much. Sometimes I found it helpful to *pray about my praying*. I asked God to help me find the words, carve out the time, find the motivation. I let God pray "through me."

Prayer is ultimately something I participate in, not manufacture. To pray is, in one sense at least, to cooperate, not force. I am not suggesting passively letting God take over. We do not become subsumed into some cosmic oversoul that diminishes our individuality. But there are times when the Spirit helps us in a way that even surpasses our expectation. In the midst of our frustrated efforts, suddenly there is an ease, a flow, a sense that we are not only praying but in some sense being prayed through.

Think of times you do something you truly enjoy. Immersed in your teaching or writing or painting, you become unaware of yourself, lost in the creative work at hand. You lose track of time, and straining ceases. You gain a glimpse of something greater than your little efforts. You become a conduit for something larger. That happens to me sometimes when I pray. The words stop mattering. They don't get in the way. Something—Someone—carries them along.

One February afternoon some years ago, that happened for me in prayer. For months—years, really—I had been praying for a breakthrough in my prayer life. I had been longing for a new spontaneity and fluency. That afternoon, as I got into my car after visiting someone from my church who was hospitalized, I started praying again about my praying. From within, it seemed, streamed an intensity of praise to God and a communion with him not bound by words. I felt a kind of electric fervor. I sensed a flowing, powerful joy. Syllables formed new combinations beyond my conscious formulations or comprehension, and they were carried along, it seemed, by a powerful force welling up within me. It was as if I were verbalizing the current from within. Some people (including me) would call this "speaking in tongues." Others less inclined to root events in the divinely supernatural would say I gave voice to a primal speech arising from subterranean depths. Careful words clearly seemed inadequate for the depth of my prayers, and God supplied the motive power and force. When Paul the apostle contrasted "praying with my mind" and "praying in the Spirit" in the New Testament, I think that is at least partly what he had in mind. The Spirit can lift our praying beyond words, carrying our hearts to a communion and undiminishable wonder that language cannot capture.

If you are growing in prayer, you will discover a deepening awareness of the divine side of the praying proposition. You will care less about articulating everything just so and, instead, open yourself more and more to the One who first comes close to us in grace and continues to help us by his presence.

⊹⟡⊹

It has been years since my son graced our family's evening prayers with his holy jabbering, years since I learned to pray through my inarticulate groans. Micah has learned to talk like any typical young man. It didn't take long, in fact, for him to give his older brother a run for his money during our family's nightly prayer routine. But I still detect in him an occasional hesitation at piecing together the words. And I still have moments when my own words (or lack of them) haven't caught up with the thoughts I want to express. Sometimes the swirl of emotions so distracts me that it is hard to find even the thoughts I might want to direct to God.

But I worry about that less than ever. I know God heard Micah's praying as a wonderful offering of honest effort. And I believe God prefers my prayers from the gut over any verbal finery. Even more significant, our desire to pray better (and to pray at all) is a sign that God has placed within us not only a desire to speak but also to pray. Our imperfect words are prompted by God and heard by him. That can free us to come to prayer, however fine or fumbling our words.

Prayers

Lord, help me not to worry about the words, but address you with the language of the heart, that my prayers, while not eloquent, will be sincere. Amen.

Lord, I do not know what to ask of you; only you know what I need. I simply present myself to you; I open my heart to you. I have no other desire than to accomplish your will. Teach me to pray. Amen.

—François Fénelon

3

A Quietness of Soul

Eloquent silence is often better than eloquent speech.

—Jewish Proverb

Silence like a poultice, comes
To heal the blows of sound.

—Oliver Wendell Holmes

In quietness and trust is [my] strength.

—Isaiah 30:15

I probably like peace and quiet as much as anyone. But I've noticed that in my commute to my office, in what could be an oasis of quiet amid life's noise and rush, I often click on the car radio. And at home after a day of meetings and ringing phones, even when supper pans have been cleaned and put away, I am prone to crank up my CD player or watch a home video. Or I think of something needing to be done—a call to make, a garbage pail to empty, an article to write. I rarely just sit in silence. I sometimes use sound and activity to avoid being alone with my thoughts.

A woman with a similar tendency once told me, "I was cross-country skiing in the Canadian Rockies. A group of us spent the day climbing high until we could see for miles the river basin and other peaks. We stood together, silent, atop a long trail we'd made through the snow. The only sounds were wind, an occasional snowbird, and the muffled noises of our beating hearts and breathing." But my friend remembers becoming uneasy. The calm was inspiring but also unsettling. "We moved on pretty quickly," she said, "with a mixture of awe and discomfort."

Sometimes we seem to need the soothing constancy of sound. We grow itchy and restless when we are with someone and the conversation lags. Driving in a car with someone we don't know well, we find the silence becoming a hollow weight. We feel an obligation to fill it with animated conversation. No wonder we gauge the success of a social evening by the energy and volume of talk. We rarely see quiet and lack of activity as an occasion for communion with another.

Or we rush around. We hurry big, sometimes for little reasons. "For too long," writes Richard Foster, "we have been in a far country: a country of noise and hurry and crowds, a country of climb and push and shove, a country of frustration and fear and intimidation."[1]

It's not that we don't, deep down, want moments of satisfying quiet. Many of us have had such moments enough to know that they can enrich us. Writer Eudora Welty tells of a time she spent sailing with the renowned novelist William Faulkner. "I was so happy he invited me," she remembers. "I don't think either of us spoke. That's all right. It was kind of magical to me. I was in the presence."[2] But quiet moments of refreshment are rare.

And even when we are alone—as we walk along a secluded wooded path, kneel alone in a chapel, or just sit on a front porch—powerful inner voices clamor for attention. The day's undone tasks cry out. Anxieties will not let us rest. There is little stillness within or around us.

No wonder we wrestle with a discipline such as prayer that takes place largely in quiet! We may decide we want to spend time with God, but we feel distracted by rush, wordiness, and emotional clutter. We want to come to God with more than a ruffled, uncollected spirit.

We want to move beyond constant chatter. So we wonder, *Is there a way through the noise? How do we silence the raging voices within?*

⊱◈⊰

One of the most profound things we can do when we talk to God is simply to sit still. Many people begin prayer with the idea that they have to say or do something—anything. I know I often come *at* God, needing to make things happen. I think I have to get things rolling.

Though I believe God does use the words of my prayers for his good purposes, though fervency and persistent asking have a hallowed place, God often intends for me to find rest or replenishment from him first. I may best begin prayer by simply pausing and letting myself *be* in God's presence. I once heard my friend Steve Brown say that he does his best praying when he *stops* praying, when he finally ceases his gabby monologue and simply waits for God.

Here is how Mark Galli, another friend, describes his discovery:

> One warm summer night I lay awake, restless and lonely for my wife and children, who were away. Rather than picking up a book or watching late-night TV—my usual lines of defense—I went outside and lay on our lawn. I started to pray but decided instead to pay attention to what was going on around me.
>
> I decided to look up. I spend most of my day focused at my level and below. At the office I see doors and windows and people and cars and the bottom half of buildings. But that night I consciously tilted my head. I saw the branches of our maple tree swaying against a sky dotted with thousands of stars.
>
> I decided to listen. I spend most of my day in my head, listening to my own agenda whirl away or, at best, hearing the words of others. Now I listened to the wind, the rustling leaves.

I decided to feel, which I rarely have time to do. The warm air glided over my skin. Grass tickled my neck. Firm ground pressed against my back.

Suddenly, and for no more than a few seconds, I experienced mystery and beauty. I glimpsed the grandeur of the universe. I felt insignificant, yet love pulsed through me, around me. I became aware of the glory of God. I lay there for many minutes, nearly in tears.

In prayer, a gentle restfulness can steal over us. Our striving ceases. We sense a gentle, loving presence. "Often," someone once told me, "I just sit in awe of God in a very content state, much like a cat on the lap of its owner." Such a "prayer of quiet" produces a new openness in the soul, a letting go of our clamoring efforts. Such times in God's presence can bring a soul-satisfying richness.

These moments may happen during an early morning prayer time. While we walk from the parking lot to our office. As we sit in the family room with our children. As we click off the bedside lamp at night. They can even permeate the day's busy activity. Sometimes while engrossed in writing a sermon or dealing with a cranky thirteen-year-old or mowing the lawn or even sitting through a business meeting that drags on, I find settling over me a calm, stilling Presence. My soul downshifts; I become suddenly aware again of the Purposeful Great Quiet of the God who pervades the universe. The stress and inner noise drop away.

⊰◈⊱

Learning quietness should not become another burdensome "project." Communion with God depends on many things, not the least of which is God's choosing to show up and set us at ease; we need him to gently help us receive what he brings. But it is also true that prayerful rest and calm do not happen by accident. Cultivating a quiet soul takes both patience and practice.

It should also be said that the goal of quiet is not the mere absence of sound. It is not to eliminate thought, as seems to be the aim in some forms of meditation and prayer influenced by Eastern religion. Rather, the goal is to make room for God's presence. To become more familiar with him. We cultivate a quiet heart because we realize that we often don't truly know people close to us (or even ourselves) because we rarely spend uncluttered time with them. It is the same with God. We create the space that allows God's sometimes whispered presence to make itself known. We practice "not doing" to allow God to do what he wants, which is usually far more than we can imagine. "Everything true and great grows in silence," writes Ladislaus Boros.[3] When we cultivate a quietness of soul, God can find room in us to dwell and speak and guide.

❖

What holds us back from cultivating quiet?

A first and obvious hindrance is that *we live in noisy, harried times.* In a video-screen-bordered world dominated by blaring volume and constant motion, calmness is seen as deadness. The popular media assaults our senses with ever louder and more frenetic images. "People haul their boom boxes to the seashore," notes Cornelius Plantinga, "so that they do not have to live in the silence between the rolling of surf and the crying of gulls, and so that no one else can live there either."[4] People who produce radio programs and movies and advertisements all seem eager to fill in our silences. They compete, sometimes mercilessly, for our attention. Much conspires against our pondering anything in quiet.

A busy wife and mother who worked outside the home once confessed to me, speaking for many of us: "I wish I had time to go off alone and quiet myself. The fact of my life is that between a husband who doesn't really understand enough to encourage my private times and the hectic pace of a taxing job, it seldom happens."

My friend knew that quiet will rarely be handed to us. To find it requires going against the grain of habit and convention. Finding it won't necessarily be easy. Sometimes when things are noisy at home and I need to rush off on an errand, I stop myself. I grab my wife, and we go for a quiet walk. Or I slow my frenzied rushing and decide to make the most of the time it takes me to get to my office or to an appointment somewhere. That is not always much, but it is something.

But I suspect that outer noise is the easiest of the obstacles to work on. Likely even tougher is this: *Quiet forces us to face ourselves in ways we would prefer to avoid.* All of us live with secret fears about ourselves. As long as my inner and outer worlds stay noisy and frenetic, I can ignore things I need to confront: my compromises, self-involvement, misgivings, unordered desires, guilt feelings, anxieties. When I am busy, when I don't listen to my deeper self, I can hide. When I am quiet, the beasts of greed or anger may rear up. It is not that they suddenly appear out of nowhere; they have lurked beneath the surface all along. But as long as I talk or fill my mind with the talk of others, I remain oblivious, and I feel falsely safe.

In all this inner disarray, I miss an opportunity. For in silence I can confront who I am, not in a threatening void, but in the presence of a loving God. Where better to make painful discoveries than in the presence of One who can forgive us and remake us?

A friend suggested to John Edward Southall, a Quaker of several generations ago, that he should learn to be still in God's presence. This, he thought, would prove an easy matter. But no sooner had he begun,

> than a perfect pandemonium of voices reached my ears, a thou-
> sand clamouring notes from without and within, until I could
> hear nothing but their noise and din. Never before did there

seem so many things to be done, to be said, to be thought, and
in every direction I was pushed and pulled and greeted with
noisy acclamations of unspeakable unrest. It seemed necessary
for me to listen to some of them, but God said, "Be still and
know that I am God." As I listened and slowly learnt to obey
and shut my ears to every sound, I found after a while that
when the other voices ceased, or I ceased to hear them, there
was a still small voice in the depths of my being that began to
speak with an inexpressible tenderness, power, and comfort.[5]

In quiet moments God can help me meet myself, my true "I,"
and lead me in grace to a place of grace and new beginnings. So I need
not ultimately fear what I will see or hear or find in the silence. That
promising prospect helps motivate me to push through the "pande-
monium" of voices and "clamouring notes."

Another hindrance to quietness, especially prominent in our
"can-do," get-it-done culture: *Withdrawing from the press of activity
seems like a waste of time, or at least a luxury.* In a world of urgent need,
of lonely senior citizens and abandoned crack babies and homeless
poor, to sit and not *do* seems self-indulgent. "Retreating" to silence
can seem like an escape from our responsibilities. So many worthy
things that need to be done scream for our attention!

Then there is *the sheer pace of our lives.* I find I'm so used to deadlines in my work, so accustomed to "efficiency" that I bring a self-
imposed urgency to everything I do. I am constantly aware of schedules and timetables and daily urgencies. So I fidget mentally in the face
of quiet. I rarely do things at a meditative pace. I rush through life. I
realize that for most of us, the greater temptations are not idle, wasted
moments and escape from responsibility but talkativeness and incessant activity.

In truth, times of quiet and withdrawal, we will find, can lead to
greater profundity, more wisdom, increased effectiveness. I like very
much the title of a book I just began reading: *In Praise of Slowness.*[6]

When we stop to think about it, we realize how essential pulling back sometimes is. How much fresher we are after a coffee break. Or how much more zest we bring to our workplaces after a few days off. Or consider an analogy: Music is beautiful not only for its notes but also for the spaces in between the notes.[7] Fewer notes, when well-placed, often make a greater impact. Likewise, you cannot have rhythm without the alternation of sound and silence. I play percussion as a hobby, and I know that, by itself, a drum roll—a continuous, blurred succession of strikes on the snare drum—hardly qualifies as stirring rhythm. It is the successive alternation of sound and silence that does. So also, "there is a time for everything…" said the ancient Hebrew writer of Ecclesiastes, "a time to be silent and a time to speak" (3:1,7). Even our daily breakfast conversations and work meetings and phone calls will have more depth and focus when we do not constantly hurry from one to the next, from one outburst of words to another. Creative withdrawal, occasional times apart to be quiet, can make all the difference. We need quiet to regather our sanity. We need healthy doses of quiet to pray well.

One desert monk in the early centuries of Christianity used a wonderful word picture: "When the door of the steambath," he said, "is continually left open, the heat inside rapidly escapes through it; likewise the soul, in its desire to say many things, dissipates its remembrance of God through the door of speech, even though everything it says may be good…. Timely silence, then, is precious, for it is nothing less than the mother of the wisest thoughts."[8] Reverential quiet, far from being a waste of time, can be a foundation for everything significant we do.

Yet another hesitancy with silent waiting on God: *Being quiet means facing God.* If we stop for a moment, we may actually hear or sense God. Perhaps we are not so sure we want to. I mean, what if God unsettles our preconceptions or prompts us to give up some things? What if, in the presence of unfathomable holiness, we experience discomfort?

But facing God in silence offers the chance of an encounter that, whatever its rough spots, ultimately leads us into the presence of Good. God's presence, his guidance, and his call not only unsettle us, but they also promise to change us for the better. "If we can pass through these initial fears and remain silent," spirituality writer Susan Muto explains, "we may experience a gradual waning of inner chaos. Silence becomes like a creative space in which we regain perspective on the whole."[9] By practicing strategic, renewing withdrawal, we may gain a glimpse of God's wider perspective.

So you are praying, lying in bed, trying to shake off sleep and start a long day, trying to concentrate on just *being* with God, when all of a sudden you receive a gentle reminder that God is present, that he will accompany you through the day's events that are about to transpire. Or as you are driving home in your car, thinking about the office and all the day's conversations, you are lifted above it all with a reassurance that allows you to calmly turn your attention to the people you are about to see at home. Or you are sitting in a church service, and it seems like Sunday morning as usual. You are fighting boredom and wishing you had had more sleep. But then a sense of peaceful calm settles over you. You realize you are being *held*. Those gifts come wrapped in silence. In the margins of quiet, we learn simply to rest in God's presence. Silence understood this way is not a temporary cessation of speech as much as an attitude of attentive alertness.

⁘⬥⁘

How do we make space for restful silence? How do we overcome the seductive pull of words and sound and motion to heed God's invitation to "be still, and know that I am God" (Psalm 46:10)?

I try to remember that much of my progress in prayer—whether in cultivating a quiet heart or learning to praise God or gaining greater comfort with spiritual things—comes as a gift. We do not tame or manipulate God by any practice or discipline. And yet we are tempted to reduce things to formulas and easily followed steps. But some things don't work that way. Cultivating a quiet heart is one.

I also try to remember that much of advancing in prayer has to do with *waiting*. Waiting is not the same as being passive. It is not doing nothing. It is readying ourselves for something more. "Be still before the LORD and wait patiently for him," Psalm 37:7 tells us. Sometimes, as the saying goes, we need to remind ourselves, "Don't just do something; sit there." *Sit.* Our goal in prayer is not to make things happen on our timetable; it is to become aware of God's presence with us. Being still in God's presence is a way to be ready.

Those who try to be faithful "listen for the sounds and silences of God," writes Cornelius Plantinga. "They quiet themselves into a kind of absorbency, a readiness to hear the word of God, and also the voice of God, and even some of the silences of God."[10] When God draws close, I want my soul to be conditioned to respond, not with grasping, but with open, gentle gratitude. I cannot do it on my own—I lack the discipline—but when I catch a glimmer of God, when he dwells with me in my prayer times, I will want to turn toward him with what John of the Cross called "a loving attention and a tranquil intellect."[11] In such moments our souls will be awakened to an awareness that, while alert, is not agitated. "The LORD is in his holy temple," wrote the Old Testament prophet when he saw God, "let all the earth be silent before him" (Habakkuk 2:20). A glimpse of God allows us to find the way to greater quiet.

❖

While silent awe before God is a gift, it can be cultivated in practical ways. If we try, I believe, simple things help us learn attentiveness, whether we spend our waking hours in an isolated office or in a house full of noisy toddlers.

I have learned, for instance, to try to have *a set-apart time*. When I can, I awake early enough to get out of bed, go to the living room, and settle in a favorite chair. I try to still the voices that rush at me, the tasks that need attention, the inner chatter that sometimes interferes with a focus on God. I try to turn the eyes of my heart to God with simple, loving intention.

When my mind wanders, I sometimes repeat a single word or phrase that helps me regain my focus. Often I simply say the name *Jesus*. Or I gently say, over and over, *Lord Jesus*. I may take a snatch of verse from the Psalms. The idea is to gently supplant the distractions with a simple, habitual focus on a phrase or word or image. This can help lead my prayer out of my noisy inner world into its quieter, truer center.

This takes practice, I find. Classical writers on the spiritual life know that when we simply try to sit still in God's presence, especially at the beginning, our minds follow old patterns. Quiet does not usually come without effort. But when we use a simple sentence such as "O God, come to my assistance" or "Your will be done" or even just "Help me, God," it is easier to let the clamor of voices and thoughts pass by without being captivated by them.

"This way of simple prayer," writes Henri Nouwen,

> when we are faithful to it and practice it at regular times,
> slowly leads us to an experience of rest and opens us to God's
> active presence. Moreover, we can take this prayer with us into
> a very busy day. When, for instance, we have spent twenty
> minutes sitting in the presence of God with the words "The
> Lord is my shepherd," they may slowly build a little nest for
> themselves in our heart and stay there for the rest of our busy
> day. Even while we are talking, studying, gardening, or build-
> ing, the prayer can continue in our heart and keep us aware of
> God's ever-present guidance.[12]

Others use a prayer of Eastern Orthodox tradition known as the Jesus Prayer (made much of by a character in J. D. Salinger's novel *Franny and Zooey*). They repeat the phrase, "Lord Jesus Christ, Son of

God, have mercy on me, a sinner." Some use a string of beads to help them continue to repeat the prayer. Often as I lie in bed in the morning, too drowsy to get up, too awake to sleep, this prayer beautifully helps my mind and heart turn to God. It helps me cut through the clutter and move from "self-consciousness to God-consciousness."[13]

A friend of mine once described his experience with the Jesus Prayer this way:

> I say the prayer in a slow, meditative way. I feel a sense of the nearness of God, that things that are weighing on my heart are being lifted up to God without my having to go verbally through the details. It's being in communion in a deep way that goes beyond words. If one of my kids is ill, instead of my having to name all the symptoms and say, "Lord, heal her," I just have a picture of her in my mind and I say, "Lord Jesus, have mercy." And it's as if I've lifted her up to the presence of Jesus. He knows far more about her condition than I could ever tell him.[14]

And although I believe the discipline of a quiet heart can and should be practiced whenever and wherever possible, I find that a designated time in the morning helps me move through the day that follows with a greater awareness and inner calm. Starting with quietness helps me continue to live with quietness.

Another way to cultivate silence is to have *a set-apart place*. Some settings are more conducive to inner quiet than others. Sometimes a particular spot can have hallowed associations for us. Our minds form a habit of associating prayer with the feel of a certain place. That can help us enter naturally into a spirit of reverence. We can claim a corner of the living room or make a simple prayer altar in our bedroom where we go simply to take refuge in prayer's restful quiet. A cross or an icon (a traditional form of religious art depicting a well-known Christian figure) sometimes helps me attend to the presence of God.

Living in a house (until recently) with three children has not always been easy, but it can be done. And when I arrive at my church office in the morning or stay late after an evening meeting, I sit in quiet for a moment and gaze out the window, or I stand in our church building and breathe in God's goodness. It helps me start my day (or end it) on a note of calm and rest rather than in frantic urgency. My office and the places I work become temporary sanctuaries.

We can also adopt *a set-apart attitude* as a way of cultivating silence. During a break time we can pull our eyes away from the day's urgencies and remember to rest quietly in the Lord's presence. We pause to draw back from the sound and fury. My friend Ann tells of a particularly difficult time at a previous job. "Sometimes it seemed all I could do just to keep my sanity." But she found that she could get through even the most stressful day by breathing a prayer of barest simplicity: "I would simply repeat the name *Jesus*. It wasn't taking his name as a swear word, but as a prayer. And it made all the difference."

You might consider "minute retreats" throughout your day. In the midst of pressing duties and a hectic pace, mentally withdraw. Take a deep breath. Put your feet up on your desk. And breathe quiet words of thanks to God.

⊹⟡⊱⟡⊰⟡⊹

A friend of mine, a practical sort, once asked about all this talk of stillness and quiet: So what difference will it make—really?

I answer with a story. Anthony Bloom, a minister and writer, tells of an elderly woman who had been working very hard at her prayers, saying them faithfully for fourteen years. But she never sensed God's presence. She came to Bloom for advice.

"I said," Bloom recounts, "'Go to your room after breakfast,... and then take your knitting and for fifteen minutes knit before the face of God, but I forbid you to say one word of prayer. You just knit and enjoy the peace of your room.'"

The woman received his counsel. At first she thought, *How nice,*

I have fifteen minutes during which I can do nothing and not feel guilty!
In time, however, she began to enter the restful quiet created by her
knitting. She became aware of God's gentle nearness. Soon, she said,
"I perceived that...at the heart of the silence there was He who is all
stillness, all peace, all poise."[15]

She had let go of her anxious, wordy efforts to meet God. And
when she did, she found God waiting.

PRAYERS

Lord, I am not good at slowing down. I like to see things
"happen." I've become hurried and harried. And I like to fill
the silences with sound.

   Draw me to the rest I find in you. Remind me that time with
you can re-create me, and fill my life with all I need. Amen.

O Lord, the Scripture says "there is a time for silence and a
time for speech." Savior, teach me the silence of humility, the
silence of wisdom, the silence of love, the silence of perfection,
the silence that speaks without words, the silence of faith.

   Lord, teach me to silence my own heart that I may listen
to the gentle movement of the Holy Spirit within me and sense
the depths which are of God.

—FRANKFURT PRAYER

O Lord, you know how busy I must be this day. If I forget you,
please do not forget me.

—GENERAL LORD ASTLEY (adapted)

THE WAY OF INTIMACY

God puts his ear so closely down to your lips that
he can hear your faintest whisper.

—THOMAS DE WITT TALMADGE

A few years ago, as I watched my mother's mind slowly unraveling, she unwittingly taught me something about prayer.

I had come from Illinois, where I lived at the time, to visit her in her Santa Monica home. I knew from earlier visits that a series of strokes had been robbing her strength and ravaging her memory. I knew from conversations with my brother, who lived just a few miles away from her, that she had declined even more since my previous visit. But I did not realize what that would mean this time.

"Do you know who I am?" I asked, leaning over the steel rails of her bed, catching the attention of her sunken eyes.

She shook her head no.

I placed before her eyes a framed picture of me as an infant I had grabbed off her maple dresser. In the picture I was chubby cheeked and smiling.

"How cute!" she said.

"Do you know who it is?"

"No."

I knew she would never again recognize me as her son.

I made small talk—the weather, my kids. But our conversation unsettled me. And as her condition worsened in the years that followed, I began to see a pattern: The more meager her response, the harder it was for me to talk. I loved her and still visited and tried to make contact, of course, but it took more willpower. People who know about such things tell us that hearing is often the last sense to go, that our loved ones who drift away from consciousness may hear and process more than we realize. But still, I sometimes wondered how much my talking to her mattered. The loss of her loving attention made me realize how much it had mattered all along.

Something similar can happen when we approach God. Nothing dampens enthusiasm for prayer like the fear of a feeble response or no response at all. Do our requests reach God's ears? Do we get through? Someone once wrote me, "One of my greatest hindrances at the beginning of my spiritual journey was feeling silly in asking and thinking that I was really talking to myself."

Worries like that nag at us as we attempt to pray. They eat away at our conviction that praying even matters. Our uncertainties hang in the air—unspoken, perhaps—but they undermine our motivation. When life gets hurried and harried, we drop whatever doesn't seem essential or fruitful. I look at my own schedule filled with an active family's activities, working at the office, writing a book in the evenings. With such demands, believing that I will get in touch with Someone who notices and knows me is the only thing that will keep me at prayer. Even a glimmer of prayer's reality will help me come to God with something approaching a regular discipline. Without that, I will be hard pressed to bother.

When we were infants, as I was in the baby picture I showed my mother, an impulse to babble happened without prompting—automatically. But the jabbering won't *continue* automatically. It has to be met with a response. In children with normal hearing—rewarded with feedback from parents—the babbling changes over time to become real language. But in deaf children who are unable to hear the normal responses, the babbling trails off. Without intervention or attention, they simply stop "trying."[1]

With no expectation of response, our praying will likewise stop. Will God pay attention? Is God too busy to hear or too far away to answer? Will we be heard? Prayer hinges on such questions. Talking to God has as much to do with the One who listens as with the one who speaks. Just as important as "how" is "Who." We need to know what will happen when we come before God.

So with my experience with my mother still on my mind, I stand back from the words and sounds and think about the climate of prayer. I find it helpful to think about my expectations.

Can I Expect God to Be Present—*Really* Present?

Merely believing in the existence of God will not inspire much enthusiasm. An analogy from life's intimate relationships shows why. Sitting in the same room only vaguely aware of your spouse or confidant or friend does not satisfy either of you for long. When my wife, Jill, and I sit in the family room, weary and distracted at the end of a long day, sometimes one of us will say, "You don't seem very present to me." If I only occupy a chair, flipping through a newspaper while she talks, I will not inspire her to share deeply.

When talking to God we likewise need to have more than a belief that God dwells "somewhere." We must know that he can be near and lend his ear. We want a very *present* God. Only the promise that I will be surrounded, held, and known makes prayer real.

I first came to this realization as a teenager. A seemingly chance campus conversation led me to the discovery that some great Someone was there. Really *there*.

It was 1969. I was fourteen, full of the unfocused energies of adolescence, caught up in the idealism of California in the late sixties. During lunch a classmate, Stan, joined me and my best friend, Don, to talk. The conversation turned to religion. Stan had become active in one of California's burgeoning churches, and, evangelical as he was, he unblushingly talked about it. My friend Don wasn't so articulate. He was the son of a Polish Jew and a Mexican Catholic (at year's end he would sign my yearbook as "The Jewish Chicano"), and to no one's surprise—including his own—he was "searching."

But Stan was uninhibited in these matters. He asked Don, "Have you ever read the Bible's New Testament?" I don't remember what Don said, but never will I forget the answer that began to form in me. It was as though someone had gently awakened me. I realized that years of church and Sunday school had left me with little firsthand acquaintance with my faith—let alone the Bible. I certainly knew little about conversing with the God I paid lip service to.

When I went home, I began making my way—page by page— through the Bible. The stories about Jesus especially captivated me. And almost immediately I became aware of a *Presence.* I had believed things *about* God, but now I began to sense—at times with a leap in my heart—that he was near, vividly so. I would awaken mornings and remember that right there, under the covers of my bed as I struggled to open my eyes, I could simply talk with God—have a conversation. I sensed that Jesus was somehow responsible for that wonderful sense of access. Who knows what made it come together at that time in my life? How can I explain why? All I know is that I became aware that I was not alone. God no longer hovered on the outer suburbs of my consciousness, to borrow an image from essayist and novelist Frederick Buechner. God had moved to the center. And because I really believed Someone was close, for the first time I prayed in more than the vaguest way.

Over the years that vivid sense of God's nearness has taken different forms, assumed varying levels of intensity or mellowness. But a conviction took root in me that has never really left me, and I have drawn on it unnumbered times. Whether in everyday moments or charged experiences of high worship, whether through snippets of prayer or intense crying out, I walk through life aware of a Presence I can address. Sometimes the awareness comes dramatically, other times gently. The Presence rarely overwhelms. But when we sense that God is close, few things seem more natural than conversation with him.

The late Simone Weil, a profound chronicler of the spiritual life, at first kept herself at a distance from God. She had developed a habit, whenever afflicted by her violent headaches, of saying the verses of George Herbert's poem "Love." She thought only that it was a beautiful poem that helped her keep her mind off her pain. But then something happened. "Without my knowing it the recitation had the virtue of a prayer," she wrote to a friend. "It was during one of these recitations that...Christ himself came down and took possession of me." In her arguments about "the problem of God," she continued, "I had never seen the possibility of...a real contact, person to person, here below, between a human being and God."[2] But then it happened. And prayer became possible.

I believe it is especially important in our time to emphasize this possibility of real conversation and contact with God. A new emphasis in some spirituality circles says that the only truly important thing is cultivating "soul" and "soulfulness." Spirituality in this vein is a vague "instinct for wonder," as easily satisfied by sitting on the south rim of the Grand Canyon as by sitting consciously in God's presence. It sounds rather spiritual but ultimately ends up quite impersonal.

This is because relationships require another *person*. Prayer requires a real God. Why work to learn the fine art of conversation and then neglect to find a friend to speak to? Who would take ballroom dancing classes but never expect to need a partner? The only reason prayer makes any sense at all is because there is Someone to talk to who will care and listen.

Perhaps more than we realize, we have all had moments of awareness of the unfathomable and ineffable that nudges us to speak and respond. We are mystics of ordinary life. I may sense God's presence while out for a morning run, driving to my office, or simply waiting in line at a supermarket checkout. We will sense him in a moment of profound stillness in a sanctuary, on a mountain drive with valleyed views that take our breath away, or during a dawning awareness that unseen arms are upholding us in a harrowing chapter in our lives. The conviction will come that around me, above me is Someone. I realize *I am not alone.*

Can We Expect God to Respond Personally?

As important as it is to realize that Someone is there, we still wonder what that "Someone" is like. My image of God—loving or vindictive, attentive or absent, kind or callous—cannot help but affect my approach to him. What if God is "there" but does not care? What if he hears but is not moved? Is he truly personal?

I regularly teach about prayer. During one such class I taught weekly for three months, I assigned "homework." "During the week ahead," I said, "jot down in a notebook your mental pictures of God."

When our class gathered next, a couple of people spoke of their perceptions of God as a kind of background Presence—vaguely there, all right, but not necessarily a *personal* Presence. Not one they could visualize as vividly personal, involved, active.

One class member, however, told of a life-changing discovery. "For a long time," she confessed, "I pictured God as a colorless blob seated on a lofty throne—like at the Lincoln Memorial." It wasn't a threatening image, but neither was it very inspiring. Then one night, she told us, she had a dream. God appeared with the shape and substance and presence of a *person*. And then it hit her: In her dream God was no longer locked in his throne room. The being once vague and distant was out walking among the people, within reach of her longing words. This change of image changed her whole approach to God. Prayer became something to which she eagerly returned.

Another person in class told of growing up under a father who, although not physically abusive, was cutting and distant. "I think I'm afraid of God in ways I'm not aware of," she told us. Memories of her hurtful father shadow her praying still. Did she secretly fear that God might be like that? Would God be mean to her?

Here I find that logical arguments for God's existence alone will do little to motivate prayer. If the God to whom such reasoning points does not attract us, if he does not come across as kind, open, welcoming, and compassionate, our praying will lack passion. The awe-inspiring Cosmic Giant must also seem capable of being our Friend. Otherwise we will hang back. Our interest in prayer will remain lukewarm.

It is no surprise, then, to find that the Bible rarely resorts to the cool, distant language of the philosopher when explaining prayer. The prophets and preachers and ordinary "everybodies" who populate the Bible's pages talk to and about God with names that come from relationships: Shepherd, Redeemer, Husband, Counselor. Their prayers have the simple but satisfying ring of conviction that Someone who cares, who stays involved, is on the other side.

I also notice that time and again the biblical writers move from the impersonal third person, *he,* to a heartfelt second person, *you.* They not only talk about God, they intimately address God. They move from mere belief to prayer. From theology to devotion. And throughout history, as someone has said, we see those who have walked the closest with God move from impersonal terms such as "the Almighty" or "the Lord God" to wonderfully comforting names, even terms of affection: Loving God, heavenly Father, Precious Lord, Breath of my breath, Hope from my youth.

Ancient religious writers so sensed this caring that they pictured God as having not only a name but a *face.* The Lord used to speak to Moses "face to face," Exodus tells us. The psalmist longed for the "face of God." This is not to say in some woodenly literalistic way that God has bristly eyebrows and a white beard. It is to say that we experience God with immediacy and intimacy. God is majestic but also accessible and loving. For Simone Weil, in the encounter described earlier,

God became real when, as she put it, "I...felt in the midst of my suffering the presence of a love, like that which one can read in the smile on a beloved face."[3]

Psychiatrist Robert Coles, in his landmark book *The Spiritual Life of Children,* was moved when he realized that of the children's 293 hand-drawn and colored pictures of God he had assigned and collected during his practice, all but 38 were of a *face*.[4] How else do we picture someone who not only exists but *cares?* God knows that whether we are young or old, rules, ideas, even ideals never satisfy our longings. Our yearnings end in a face.

That is why Christians make so much of Jesus: In him people meet a God who took on the contours and lines and gestures of human expression, who assumed a human form to walk along the roads and dusty detours of human life. A God who incredibly, unbelievably suffered to allow his own Son to be hung on a cross in first-century Palestine to wash away forever the notion that anything could keep God far away.

"I need more than words," I have heard people say, "I need a God with 'skin.'" The God we sometimes picture as enshrouded in mist carries a name and shows a caring countenance.

How does this become more than mere proposition and head knowledge? Not through arduous philosophizing. Our questions about God are ultimately matters of relationship, not rationalism. They have more to do with our hearts than our heads.

A Pakistani woman named Bilquis Sheikh discovered this:

> Suddenly, a breakthrough of hope flooded me. Suppose, just suppose God were like a father. If my earthly father would put aside everything to listen to me, wouldn't my heavenly Father...?
>
> Shaking with excitement, I got out of bed, sank to my knees on the rug, looked up to heaven and in rich new understanding called God "My Father."

I was not prepared for what happened....

Hesitantly, I spoke his name aloud. I tried different ways of speaking to him. And then, as if something broke through for me I found myself trusting that he was indeed hearing me, just as my earthly father had always done.

"Father, O my Father God," I cried, with growing confidence. My voice seemed unusually loud in the large bedroom as I knelt on the rug beside my bed. But suddenly that room wasn't empty any more. *He* was there! I could sense his presence. I could feel his hand laid gently on my head. It was as if I could *see* his eyes, filled with love and compassion. He was so close that I found myself laying my head on his knees like a little girl sitting at her father's feet. For a long time I knelt there, sobbing quietly, floating in his love. I found myself talking with him, apologizing for not having known him before. And again, came his loving compassion, like a warm blanket settling around me.[5]

The sentence humankind craves to hear, says novelist and essayist Reynolds Price, is, "The Maker of all things loves and wants me."[6] That expresses our deep hope. I believe this is precisely why the Bible so often uses parental imagery for God. When Jesus's disciples asked him how to pray, the first thing in his model prayer (known now as the Lord's Prayer) drew on the language of familial relationship: Our Father.

Ah, but it is one thing for *Jesus* to address God with the license of parent-child interaction. If anyone could, it would be *him*. But does that mean we can? Jesus also taught that *we, too,* can address God with the language of family intimacy. "*Your* Father knows what you need before you ask him," he once told his audience of disciples and curious onlookers (Matthew 6:8, emphasis added). And he told us to come to God in that very way, to address him as Father.

It is true that for some who have been abused and harassed by earthly fathers, the fatherly image does not evoke warm, nurturing memories, but rather, horror. An abusive earthly father does not an inviting picture make. But the idea is to take the image of an ideal father and blow it up large. For Jesus takes all that is good and rich in the image of human parenting and fathering and applies it to our relationship to God. At one point he even encourages us to call God *Abba,* an Aramaic term akin to *Daddy* in English, which is akin to a child's first efforts to address his father: *Dada.*

Jesus is not suggesting sentimental childishness in our relationship with God—no. But trusting child*like*ness, yes. He is unflinchingly insisting that we can address the same great Creator and Sustainer of all with the winsome intimacy of a child with his or her parents. Perhaps that is why wherever the New Testament speaks of requests being made to God, it emphasizes that God hears them.[7] It emphasizes God's caring involvement.

When I was very young, perhaps four or five, I would often sit with my mother. She had an old, rock-hard maple rocking chair, and I would climb onto her lap while she held me and rocked me. Sometimes she sang children's ditties like "Froggy Went a Courtin'." I was held tightly and felt safe. I could tell her when a bully was scaring me or a fall had bruised me. Sometimes I needed to ask something or just express my own childlike affection. I knew I had her attention.

That is how it is with prayer. God does not forget us. Nothing impairs his hearing. It is this conviction—or even faltering hope—that helps us pray. When we believe that we are heard, we will pray. When we have even the faintest hope that someone will respond, we will have the courage to keep praying. And nothing will hold us back. Whatever words I may reverently utter or simply fling God's way, whatever struggle I sometimes have in sensing him, the reality that makes it all worth it is that God himself is listening.

PRAYERS

Lord, sometimes I wonder if you hear my prayers. But at other times I am amazed at how quickly you listen and how surely you respond. Help my trust in your relentless tenderness to grow. Amen.

Heavenly Father, you have promised to hear what we ask in the Name of your Son: Accept and fulfill our petitions, we pray, not as we ask in our ignorance, nor as we deserve in our sinfulness, but as you know and love us in your Son Jesus Christ our Lord. Amen.

—THE BOOK OF COMMON PRAYER

Now to him who is able to do immeasurably more than all we ask or imagine, according to his power that is at work within us, to him be glory in the church and in Christ Jesus throughout all generations, for ever and ever! Amen.

—EPHESIANS 3:20-21

PART II

WHAT WE
SAY

FACING OUR FAILINGS:
CONFESSION AND REPENTANCE

Our courteous Lord does not want his servants to despair
even if they fall frequently and grievously. Our falling does
not stop his loving us.

—JULIAN OF NORWICH, *Revelations of Divine Love*

If the Spirit of God detects anything in your life that is
wrong, He does not ask you to put it right; He asks you to
accept the light, and He will put it right. A child of the
light confesses instantly and stands bared before God; a
child of the darkness says—Oh, I can explain that away.

—OSWALD CHAMBERS, *My Utmost for His Highest*

The prayer preceding all prayers is "May it be the real I
who speaks. May it be the real Thou that I speak to."

—C. S. LEWIS, *Letters to Malcolm:
Chiefly on Prayer*

D uring one year in college, I met with a small group every week.
We ranged from young-adult singles to grandparents, engineers
to homemakers, but we all wanted to grow spiritually. One evening
we explored the practice of admitting our faults to God through

confession. The discussion made someone I'll call Jeff fidgety. He finally blurted out, "I just don't understand all this. I'm a good person! I don't have anything to confess!"

I have never forgotten Jeff's puzzlement: He did not bilk senior citizens of life savings or sell crack cocaine. Why the need to pray about failings? The idea was foreign, even offensive. He seemed untroubled by conscience or compunction.

But next consider someone I'll call Jennifer, whom I met years later. When we talked, her husband had grown sullen and distant. Communication had ground to a standstill. As if the emotional barrenness (and abuse) at home were not enough, shame over her failing marriage kept Jennifer from turning to friends for comfort. Because divorce loomed, and her upbringing made her see divorce as almost unforgivable, Jennifer felt she was angering God. Guilt consumed her. She stopped praying. "I'm afraid that God won't hear my prayer. I feel unworthy, and it's driving me further from God." Far from feeling oblivious to guilt, she was paralyzed by it.

Between these two stories lies yet another, a composite of people I have talked to over the years, people who constantly try to shake the nagging feeling that they don't "measure up." "I don't go to church enough," they sometimes say. Or "I spend too little time with my kids." Sometimes the pricks on conscience come from something more serious: failing to walk away when their employer dabbles in morally dubious activities. Perhaps they remember errant sexual activities from the past. Guilt hounds their consciences. It does not debilitate, but it certainly makes them miserable. It robs life of joy.

However guilt affects us, in whichever story we see ourselves, confession belongs in prayer. Admitting who we are and are not, what we have done and have not done, all form part of a healthy conversation with God. Practicing such honest disclosure gives us an outlet for processing what we think are slip-ups and indiscretions as well as "big" sins. Admitting in prayer what plagues my conscience or nags at my peace or destroys my relationships with others helps me deal with places that need forgiveness and purifying. I am learning that confessing is a wonderful way to keep my relationship with God clean and uncluttered. Confession is where my tender conscience and the love of God meet. And because confession ultimately involves both our feelings and God's response, I am finding that several important things happen in and through it.

Sometimes Confession Is as Simple as Admitting Before God That Our Self-Involvement Does Not Fit Reality

We need to see our proper place on occasion. A psychiatrist, the joke goes, tells a client, "No, you don't have an inferiority complex. You really *are* inferior." Well, we are less than God. We will never run the risk of eclipsing him. We won't qualify as God impersonators—nor do we want to, when we think about it.

And in the presence of God's unfathomable greatness, it takes effort (or a huge ego) to avoid feeling small and incomplete. We inhabit a cosmos, I'm told, in which a dime held at arm's length before the night sky would block fifteen million stars from view, if our eyes could see with that power. The sheer vastness of the universe does not let us long swagger in self-importance.

No wonder the psalm writer, scratching his head in wonderment, penned,

> When I consider your heavens,
>   the work of your fingers,
> the moon and the stars,
>   which you have set in place,
> what is man that you are mindful of him? (8:3-4)

When we confess our smallness to God, we are simply reaffirming what reality would tell us daily, if we had a proper view. There can be wonderful freedom in this. If you or I represent a speck under the unimaginably deep canopy of the starry heavens, if one life is a blip in the grand sweep of world history, the burden of having to "do it all" lifts. We see that we are not the only ones who matter, and the million things screaming for our attention, the mounds of tasks that make us feel indispensable, suddenly lose some of their power. As we gain a proper perspective on the larger scope of things, we relax a little. Confessing my smallness puts life—and my pride—in perspective.

So when I wander under a night sky or sit on the shore before an ocean panorama or just sit in a comfortable room to pray, I see glimmers of the Great One who inhabits eternity. It helps me pray with appropriate humility. I find it easier not to think of myself more highly than I ought. And that glimpse of my place only magnifies God's amazing willingness to notice me, smallness and all.

But even though confession represents recognizing what is already reality—though it makes sense—admitting our moral smallness also leaves us uncomfortable. Sometimes it goes against our inclinations; confession requires resolve. Which leads us to another truth.

Confession Asks That We Recognize
Our Incompleteness—and That Can Be More Difficult

We often prefer our illusion of self-mastery and control. I live in a world of the well-fed, well-dressed, and well-presented. But under my niceness and attention to appearances lurks an inner world of envy and ambition and seething hurts. I have things in my life I would like to hide.

Years ago a story from novelist Harry Crews's memoir, *A Childhood,* reminded me of this in an especially powerful way. He was remembering his poor rural Georgia upbringing and the Sears, Roebuck catalog:

> I first became fascinated with the Sears catalog because all the people in its pages were perfect. Nearly everybody I knew had something missing, a finger cut off, a toe split, an ear half-chewed away, an eye clouded with blindness from a glancing

fence staple. And if they didn't have something missing, they were carrying scars from barbed wire, or knives, or fishhooks. But the people in the catalog had no such hurts. They were not only whole, had all their arms and legs and toes and eyes on their unscarred bodies, but they were also beautiful…and on their faces were looks of happiness, even joy, looks I never saw much of in the faces of the people around me.

Young as I was, though, I had known for a long time that it was all a lie. I knew that under those fancy clothes there had to be scars, there had to be swellings and boils of one kind or another because there was no other way to live in the world.[1]

For all its seeming appeal, protecting the veneer of rightness robs life of liberating honesty. Our personal myths of near perfection bring stiffness to relationships. We work so hard at looking good and smelling sweet that we rarely act natural or become truly transparent. We indulge in what political commentator Joe Klein calls "lawyering the truth."[2]

When we try to hide our incompleteness from God, we make relating to him nearly impossible. I once heard a friend say, "When I was growing up, I was always the 'good kid,' and I guess I bring the pressure from that into my relating to God. I find I often don't bring to God the gut-wrenching things going on in my life. I'm sometimes afraid to say, 'Lord, this is what I'm really like.'" But how valuable when we push through our initial reluctance!

One-time Nixon "hatchet man" Charles Colson learned this. In the wake of the Watergate scandal, he did some profound soul "inventorying." Then Colson visited a friend who tried to help Colson face squarely what he had done. The friend shared words about pride being a kind of spiritual cancer that eats up the "very possibility of love or contentment." "Suddenly," Colson wrote, "I felt naked and unclean, my bravado defenses gone. I was exposed, unprotected.…

[His words about pride] seemed to sum up what had happened to all of us at the White House....." Colson couldn't shake the impact of his friend's tough words:

> Outside in the darkness, the iron grip I'd kept on my emotions began to relax. Tears welled up in my eyes as I groped in the darkness for the right key to start my car....
>
> As I drove out of Tom's driveway the tears were flowing uncontrollably. There were no streetlights, no moonlight. The car headlights were flooding illumination before my eyes, but I was crying so hard it was like trying to swim underwater. I pulled to the side of the road not more than a hundred yards from the entrance to [my friend's] driveway.... I remember hoping that [my friend] wouldn't hear my sobbing, the only sound other than the chirping of crickets that penetrated the still of the night. With my face cupped in my hands, head leaning forward against the wheel, I forgot about machismo, about pretenses, about fears of being weak. And as I did, I began to experience a wonderful feeling of being released. Then came the strange sensation that water was not only running down my cheeks, but surging through my whole body as well, cleansing and cooling as it went. They weren't tears of sadness and remorse, nor of joy—but somehow, tears of relief. And then I prayed my first real prayer.[3]

Confession provides a way to slice through our defenses. It reminds us of our utter freedom to be incomplete before God. With God we can lay aside our shielding pride. When my perfectionism drives me always to be more and do more, I turn to God in my disappointment. I find comfort in admitting my limits before God. "I know what I am," I say in prayer. "I admit it: I do not have it all together."

Above All, Confession Means
Facing Hard into Our Moral Failings

Through confession we express our regret. We come, faults and all, not rationalizing or hiding or masking who we are. We admit not only that we sin but that we are sinners. That at the root of our lives, we are "bent" away from God. We admit, perhaps with tears, that we love the things of self and yawn in the awesome presence of God. We acknowledge that we obsess about our whims and recoil from self-sacrifice.

It is this dimension of confession perhaps that most goes against the grain of our culture. The mood of our times prefers a sunny view of human nature. Terms such as *sin* and *vice* have fallen out of fashion. You never hear them on the six o'clock news. In all kinds of settings, we shave corners and bend rules but prefer not to own up to our self-indulgent screwups. In office buildings across the country, millions of people put up a Teflon exterior in the hope that when a project goes sour, no guilt will stick. Or marriages drift toward divorce when neither spouse will admit to acting like a spoiled child.

But our stubborn insistence upon always being right comes with its own costs. We expend huge amounts of energy rationalizing wrongs and justifying missteps. Just as bad, our stubborn refusal to be wrong drives us to blame others—or anything. We make ourselves out as victims and then complain about the other guy. We feed a cycle of accusation and counteraccusation. We even blame impersonal forces. When we fail, says Edmund in Shakespeare's *King Lear,* even due to our own shortcomings, "we make guilty of our disasters the sun, the moon, and stars, as if we were villains [by] necessity...drunkards, liars, and adulterers by an enforced obedience of planetary influence."[4] We prefer to lay the onus on the stars or our genes or our parents—anything to avoid seeing ourselves as flawed and anemic in virtue.

The words *good* and *evil,* noted a writer in *Newsweek,* "are often deemed too judgmental for public discourse. Even from pulpits, sin receives only mumbled acknowledgment."[5] But such categories help us name what we sense on a deep level to be true. Our guilt has gritty basis in reality. We are part of a fallen race. The theologians call it original sin. We are not mistaken when we see sin in ourselves. "All have sinned," the Scripture says, "and fall short of the glory of God" (Romans 3:23). If we dig around in the compost of our psyches long enough, we cannot long avoid the moldering whiffs.

When I am honest, I find plenty to fill my own moments of confession. One morning not long ago, as I stood in my bathroom shaving and readying myself for the day, I realized with a wave of sadness how preoccupied I am with my own needs. Even my nobler projects— writing a book on prayer, preaching sermons that people tell me help them, raising a family—are interwoven with ambition and with my constant interest in *me*. Rarely do I ever rise above self. Daily relationships are marred by concern about how I compare with others. Even when I come to God, I'm thinking about what he can do for me.

My friend Kevin told me of a powerful prayer time he had recently. "Unusual for me, I spent most of my prayer time last Saturday confessing. It wasn't a maudlin affair. I simply realized how the whole of my life seems to center around work, around my success. The inner forces seem centripetal, throwing me inward, not centrifugal, throwing me outward to connect with others." Kevin did not consciously list infractions; it was more like pondering what he *was* in the presence of God. It was seeing afresh the fundamental direction of his life while saying, "Yes, Lord, what you're showing me is true." It was recognizing that without a front-end alignment, he might end up in a ditch.

In our alienation from others, our lashing out at the innocent, our sensualism and gluttony (you name the sin), we need confession, which means, in its most literal sense, "to agree with, to admit as true." When we confess, we agree with God that we are fallen creatures prone to wandering. We admit that we transgress his moral law and ignore our consciences. To understand the horrors that fill the headlines of our newspapers, to confront the dark impulses that drive and tempt us, we need more than a sociology textbook. We need God's reality check and his redemptive promises.

I have recently been reading *All Rivers Run to the Sea,* the moving memoirs of Elie Wiesel, novelist and Nobel laureate. He recounts the horrors of the concentration camps of Nazi Germany, perhaps the most notorious example of human evil of the last century. As a fifteen-year-old, when Elie and his family arrived at the Birkenau camp in Poland, the men and women were immediately separated. Even now, decades later, he cannot believe what he witnessed:

> It's only a dream, I told myself as I walked, hanging on my
> father's arm. It's a nightmare that they have torn me from
> those I love, that they are beating people to death, that Birke-
> nau exists and that it harbors a gigantic altar where demons
> of fire devour our people. It's in God's nightmare that human
> beings are hurling living Jewish children into the flames.[6]

We are not mistaken when we sorrow over evil. It is not a dream. From the hideous crimes of a Pol Pot or Hitler to the pesky meanness of a racist neighbor, we cannot deny evil's reality. And when we scrutinize our own consciences, we see our own complicity and compromises with evil. We face all this when we confess. In doing so we face down our avoidance. For to unflinchingly face our sin is the beginning of our victory over its power to hold us back and keep us from God. "The man who knows his sins," said desert monk Isaac the Syrian centuries ago, "is greater than one who raises a dead man by his prayer."[7]

So as you grow in prayer and sanctity, do not be surprised if your recourse to confession increases. The more you rest in the presence of God, the more your imperfections may stand out. The nearer you stand to dazzling white, the harder it is to ignore the stains on your soul. In the radiant health of God our desperate need for others' approval will look like an itchy sore.

It is no accident that when the prophet Isaiah had a vision of the Lord "seated on a throne," he immediately felt compelled to cry, "Woe to me!... I am a man of unclean lips, and I live among a people of unclean lips, and my eyes have seen the King, the LORD Almighty" (Isaiah 6:1,5).

In Confessing We Find a Way Through Guilt
On the other side of our coming clean with God lies not doleful dreariness but release and undreamed-of wholeness.

Confession, and where it leads us, may sometimes show us that our guilty consciences are not always infallible. Sometimes our guilt does not have a basis in fact. Most of us, I believe, have within us what I once heard someone call a sea of guilt. When we do something that does not even remotely meet the expectations of those around us, the waves of remorse may wash over us. A woman may feel she must be a faultless cook and housekeeper, an always-available mother, a rising-star executive, and an effervescent companion for her husband—all at once. She is caught up in a cross fire of roles and cultural expectations no one person can hope to fulfill.

Or a man may unconsciously hark back to when he was a child trying to please a domineering parent. He secretly hopes that his careful compliance with the demands of his bosses will keep peace. When someone frowns or expresses annoyance, he frantically turns inward to find the fault that caused the breach. His overly sensitive conscience leads him not to God but to introspection and self-absorption. Guilt becomes a disease that renders him a spiritual invalid. He hasn't done something wrong; he is experiencing what some call pseudoguilt.

In such situations confession can have a healing role. It frees us from the mire of self-recrimination so that we can breathe the fresh air of grace. Even the smallest trifle, if it makes us feel uncomfortable or guilty, should be brought before God in prayer. If it should turn out to be pseudoguilt, then our time in the healing presence of God will reveal that. The guilt will drop away. Each time of confession before God will serve to develop in us healthier patterns of relating and reacting.

Confession should not ever leave us stuck in despair. We do not need to wallow in guilt. The dis-ease we *should* feel when we do wrong drives us into the arms of God. Then our guilt rises between us and God not as a wall but as a bridge.

> When I kept silent,
>   my bones wasted away
>   through my groaning all day long.
> For day and night
>   your hand was heavy upon me;
> my strength was sapped
>   as in the heat of summer.
> Then I acknowledged my sin to you
>   and did not cover up my iniquity.
> I said, "I will confess
>   my transgressions to the LORD"—
> and you forgave
>   the guilt of my sin. (Psalm 32:3-5)

So it is true, each of us may know on a feeling level that sin separates us from God. Sin leaves us immersed in self and turned away from him. But God overcomes its effects. Our sense of unworthiness does not need to keep us from God. Instead, it can open us to our need for God's mercy like nothing else. "This is love:" we read in the Bible, "not that we loved God, but that he loved us and sent his Son as an atoning sacrifice for our sins" (1 John 4:10).

In some primal, mysterious way, Jesus took upon himself the evil and hostility of all time and redeemed it on the cross. His blood became our peace. His broken body our hope. He reconciled us to God. He restored what had been shattered. "This is that mystery," said Martin Luther centuries ago, "which is rich in divine grace unto sinners: wherein by a wonderful exchange, our sins are no longer ours but Christ's; and the righteousness of Christ is not Christ's but ours. He has emptied himself of his righteousness that he might clothe us with it, and fills us with it: and he has taken our evils upon himself that he might deliver us from them."[8] God will not let our guilt stand between us and him, if we are willing to let him wash it away.

Out of his graciousness, God invites us to come, warts (and worse) and all. He does not demand perfection, only a "broken and contrite heart" (Psalm 51:17). Because of what he has done and told us in Jesus Christ, we do not shrink back or come to him with our guard up. We come humbly, but we also know that we will not be laughed out of the throne room. We come with "freedom and confidence," as Paul the apostle tells us in Ephesians 3:12.

As we grow in our relationship with God, we will find him gently revealing things we need to acknowledge, seek forgiveness for, and turn from. "Last week I said something flip and damaging about somebody I know," a friend recently told me. "Within twenty-four hours I had one of those 'ding' moments when, with the clarity of a bell ringing, I realized that what I had said was unfair." God has a way of pointing out our failings without our doing a lot of mournful probing.

When I feel guilty, or don't feel guilty but sense I should, I know how to pray. I turn to God for forgiveness. I see how grace, not my performance, is what matters. And that gives me great courage, even knowing that I will sometimes falter and perhaps fail.

PRAYERS

Have mercy on me, O God,
according to your unfailing love;
according to your great compassion
blot out my transgressions.

Wash away all my iniquity
and cleanse me from my sin.
For I know my transgressions,
and my sin is always before me....
Create in me a pure heart, O God,
and renew a steadfast spirit within me.
Do not cast me from your presence
or take your Holy Spirit from me.
Restore to me the joy of your salvation
and grant me a willing spirit, to sustain me.

—PSALM 51:1–3, 10–12

Come, let us to the Lord our God
With contrite hearts return;
Our God is gracious, nor will leave
the desolate to mourn.

—JOHN MORISON, EIGHTEENTH CENTURY

Enjoying God:
Praise and Thanksgiving

A single grateful thought raised to heaven is
the most perfect prayer.

—Gotthold Ephraim Lessing

Adoration is the lifting up of the heart and mind to God,
asking nothing but to enjoy God's presence.

—*The Book of Common Prayer*

One early morning not long ago, I sat down with a list of concerns. I tried—earnestly—to pray. Toward the top of the list were my wife and kids, my brother and his family. Farther down was the name of a friend who was writing a book and needed all the wisdom and help he could get. And how could I forget the war raging overseas? Two dozen items called out for my attention. But something wasn't right. It could have been my sluggish, drowsy mind. (It was, after all, *very* early.) Or perhaps my distracted worrying over a project at work (which was what had awakened me in the first place). But more than anything, I think I simply needed prayer that morning to go beyond asking. Something in me wanted to rise above my prayer "agenda." I had first to silence my unquiet mind and give voice to something even deeper than need.

While concern for our lives' gritty needs may drive us to God, it can also sabotage our praying. The urgency and desire to see things "happen" that drive us to our knees can also drive us to distraction. Our souls can become cluttered with what someone has called "much-ness and manyness." A friend of mine once said, "I come to prayer like I do to a fast-food restaurant instead of to elegant dining. And my spirit is becoming malnourished." If *all* I do is ask, I may only become more agitated. Prayer becomes an urgent transaction rather than an encounter with the living God.

When prayer becomes as hurried and hassled as our nine-to-five lives, we cover ground but rarely stand on holy ground. While we pray for the things we want to see changed, we also remember to pause and consider who we're talking to. While I believe I should ask—earnestly and without guilt—I frequently find myself redis-covering another side to prayer that can be even more profound and life-changing. My spiritual sanity cannot do without time for lovingly pondering and enjoying God.

As I take time to enjoy God, I find myself lifted out of life's littleness. I become caught up in a vision of Someone who captures the attention of the profoundest longings of my soul. One writer calls it the "cultivated habit of looking up and away from myself."[1] It is cul-tivating the habit of coming to God ready to enjoy God. I stand back from the striving and talking in order to remember the wonderful Reality whom I address.

❖

"What is the chief end of humankind?" asks the venerable West-minster catechism. Generations of schoolchildren have learned the concise answer: "To glorify God and *enjoy* him forever" (emphasis added). Significant things happen when we simply gaze prayerfully, gladly in God's direction. The power driving our desperately urgent agendas may wane. Our concerns about our world may pale next to the One who inhabits the heavens. We learn to take time out of our busy schedules to enjoy our great and wonderful God. "One day," my friend Marge told me, "I was praying. I heard a small, inaudible, but very distinct [statement], 'Stop trying so hard.' I had trouble believing what I was being told, so I asked God, 'Then how do you want me to pray?' I don't remember whether I got an answer or what I did. But I *relaxed*. I started paying attention to *God*. Since then, I have learned how important it is to allow myself simply to be in his presence."

I can recall many times when on a morning run or during late-night prayer, I simply meditated on God. During such times I think gently of his presence. I don't try to say much. I try gratefully to "be still," as the psalm says, "and know that [he is] God" (46:10). When I conclude my prayer times, I sometimes feel a vague uneasiness that I haven't brought to mind many requests. A number of important stones have gone unturned. But there steals over me an even stronger, profounder sense of being "done," of prayer having done its work.

The power of spending gentle, joyous time in God's presence comes from the recognition that he is great, that my soul will find much to feed on. We can be, as one writer suggests, "fascinated" with God. "We admire athletes for their strength and musicians for their talents. The abilities of the sculptor amaze us. The charisma of the statesman fascinates us. Yet, we are so seldom fascinated with God.... Prayer is an excellent means of refreshing our appreciation for God."[2]

But there is more. To our simple enjoyment of God we add awe and wonder.

We live in times, pastor Donald Shelby likes to say, that are more characterized by "Blah" than "Ah!" I would add that we don't do well when it comes to *awe,* either. Our souls may need practice in cultivating this attention to grandeur. We need our capacity for quiet amazement expanded, for we tend to project our jaded outlooks onto God. We think small and expect little. No wonder Elizabeth Barrett Browning wrote,

Earth's crammed with heaven,
And every common bush afire with God;
But only he who sees, takes off his shoes,
The rest sit round it and pluck blackberries.[3]

But God is bigger and better than our imaginations can conceive. In a universe brimming with the unfathomable, the soul's appropriate stance is amazed reverence. God still shows up on the scene as more than a vague force; he appears before us as glorious and wonderfully strange.

One simple way to remember this is to sit quietly in a forest, or watch the clouds dance on a blustery fall day, or stand in the spray of a waterfall, or walk an urban street after new snowfall has scoured the city's grime with its gentle white. The glories of nature point to the glory of God. They help us think about the hand behind the handiwork, the miraculous power behind the marvel. "The heavens declare the glory of God," said David of Israel. "The skies proclaim the work of his hands. Day after day they pour forth speech" (Psalm 19:1-2).

For all the grandeur and dazzle of the universe's natural wonders, there is something even greater that inspires grateful awe: the crown of God's creation, humankind. We are "fearfully and wonderfully made," as the psalmist put it (Psalm 139:14). We see such wonder-filled evidence in so many glimpses: the charged intimacy of romantic love, the heroic compassion of a saint, the simple pleasure of conversing with a friend. All such reminders of the goodness of God's creation in humankind point to a Creator who is eminently, irresistibly worthy of our reverence. He saturates our human life with his creative genius.

When we see the wonders of earth and humankind, when we remember that God *made* us and controls creation still, we realize his glory all the more. The most awe-inspiring vista, the most breathtaking mountain scene, the most powerful natural force all point not to themselves but to a God who holds them easily in his hands.

I know that the LORD is great,
    that our Lord is greater than all gods.
The LORD does whatever pleases him,
    in the heavens and on the earth,
    in the seas and all their depths.
He makes clouds rise from the ends of the earth;
    he sends lightning with the rain
    and brings out the wind from his storehouses.
        (Psalm 135:5-7)

As important as living with a sense of wonder is, this does not exhaust our celebration of God. In many ways, such awe-infused prayer is only the beginning of our adoration. While we admire the heavens, the seas, and the mountains, nature cannot meet our need for intimacy, our longing to *express* our awe. Redwood forests and sunsets move us, but as objects of worshipful love, they fail, no matter how breathtaking they are. A woman who had given up on religious faith was hiking amid the beauty of the Swiss Alps. She wrote to a friend, "I long to make some small sound of praise to someone, but whom?" We need some*one* to adore.

Wonder, therefore, gives way to another impulse of the praying heart: praise. We say not only "What beauty!" but also "What a great God!" We do more than bask in the sunshine. "One's mind," as C. S. Lewis wrote, "runs back up the sunbeam to the sun."[4] We give our wonder a name, and we praise the source. When we come to God with adoration, it is not so much for what he has created as for *who he is*. We worship and love him for himself. We honor and glorify him who has existed from eternity.

The biblical record is replete with praise and adoration, as this example from the Psalms shows:

> I will exalt you, my God the King;
>   I will praise your name for ever and ever.
> Every day I will praise you
>   and extol you name for ever and ever.
>
> Great is the LORD and most worthy of praise;
>   his greatness no one can fathom. (145:1-3)

In the New Testament alone, the passages that urge or describe praise and thanksgiving number well over two hundred. The words take on astonishing variety: *bless, worship, glorify, magnify, extol,* to name just a few. They all point to the fact that as we see God for who he is, our response is rightly one of adoring worship. When faced with such grandeur, we bend the knee and bow in reverence.

Praise can be a constant in our praying, even as other aspects of our lives shake or crumble. Some years ago my wife went through a particularly dismal and discouraging time. She was feeling stung by criticism from a handful of members of the church where we were on the pastoral staff. She brought her hurt easily to her prayers. But then she began to cut through her pain by doing something that seemed almost irrational: She filled her praying with praise. Far from sensing that she was living in denial, she felt more whole, more *herself,* more like she was doing what she was made to do. The goodness of God to us emerged as the true reality. The Bible's depictions of God as trustworthy, sufficient, loving, mighty, steadfast, generous, able, merciful, truthful, and victorious all became sources of bedrock hope for us. Together in our praying we heeded the biblical summons to fill our prayers with recognition of God's immutable goodness.

This emphasis on praise, however, leaves in some people's minds a question: If God is God, why should he care whether we honor him with our praises? "When I first began to draw near to belief in God," wrote C. S. Lewis, "I found a stumbling block in the demand so clamorously made by all religious people that we should 'praise' God; still more in the suggestion that God Himself demanded it.… It was hideously like saying, 'What I most want is to be told that I am great and good.'"[5] After all, we despise a man or woman who, in seeming insecurity, insists on being complimented.

But when we call a painting "admirable," reflected Lewis, we mean that admiration is the correct or appropriate response. That if we praise such a work, it will not be senseless or out of touch with reality. Indeed, not to do so may indicate more about our crude insensitivity than anything else. Praise, then, is not just a subjective whim; it is God's due. It is expected. It is right. We fall short if we, curmudgeonlike, withhold it.

And because appreciation, love, and delight all strive for an outlet or object, to keep our enjoyment in God's presence unarticulated or unnoticed diminishes us. Bottled up, the impulse to praise will grow faint. Unexpressed, it may shrink our souls. It will languish, just as love for another person never expressed will always be a frustrated love. To praise that which is praiseworthy does something in us. And the more worthy the object, the more exalted our appreciation, the more intense our delight in expressing it.

❖

Wonder and praise do not yet exhaust our repertoire of enjoying God. When we glory in who God is, we not only praise him for his immutable being, we thank him for particular blessings. Here again, we can use practice.

Whatever you make of the thesis of the book *The Culture of Complaint,* the title speaks volumes. It is more fashionable to grouse and pretend that nothing and no one can satisfy. But a dulled, blasé outlook robs our praying of its power. I have a friend who recently concluded that his thinking and praying have been too much laced with discontent. Now he wants to replace his murmuring with an "attitude of gratitude." I know what he means. I find it easy to dwell in prayer on what I need but neglect to mention with thankful breath what I already have received. I let daily pressures so consume my waking life that I forget the gentle joy of living thankfully.

Making thankfulness a fixture in our daily outlook is not always easy. Some years ago my friends Jeff and Diane faced a tragedy. Within hours of giving birth to their first child, a doctor told them that tiny Joshua was "underdeveloped and retarded." Diane remembers the first night after the diagnosis: "It was a sleepless time, with the word *retarded* echoing all night. It seemed like a nightmare."

Jeff faced his struggle the next day. He had long before promised the Ohio congregation where he was a student-pastor that he would drive out and let them know when the baby was born. He would get the word out, he had said, by ringing the church's steeple bell. "When I was wrestling with why this had happened to me," Jeff told me, "I thought, *I don't want to ring the bell.*" After all, bells had to do with *good* news. But what do you do in the midst of disappointment?

After an early morning time of grief and wrestling in prayer, Jeff knew what to do: "I got cleaned up and changed, ate breakfast, and made a beeline for the church. I decided to ring the bell."

Hearing Jeff and Diane talk about Joshua, now a cherished, strapping young man of twenty, made me think of Paul the apostle's words in the New Testament: "Give thanks in all circumstances" (1 Thessalonians 5:18). On the surface, such advice seems to run counter to all reason. But when we learn the fine art of living gratefully, we thank God even for life's sometimes hidden or disguised blessings. God gives us the ability to be grateful even when things are hard. We are able to ring steeple bells even in sadness.

Grief and inconvenience are not our only challenges to living and praying thankfully. Our daily routines can get us out of the habit of thankfulness. Sometimes I stop and think of all I have to be grateful for, and I become amazed at how oblivious I've become. My wife narrowly missed serious—potentially fatal—injury when the car's accelerator got stuck. When she told me afterward about her harrowing maneuvering through busy intersections—without mishap—I was filled with gratefulness that she was fine. But why wasn't I that thankful for her all along?

Some years ago a nasty software virus put my computer out of commission for the better part of a week. When I got it back from the shop, how grateful I was to sit down and use it once again and realize almost none of my files had been lost. Why wasn't I grateful for my computer before I almost lost it all?

Simple distractions also war against a thankful attitude. When you are barely holding on amid the stress of great demands, it is not always easy to feel thankful. My friend Marge has an antidote. "When I get distracted or I 'dry up' spiritually, I simply sit in my 'prayer spot'—a chair in the corner of my living room by a window. And if I'm having trouble, I look out the window and start with prayers of simple thanksgiving—for the diamonds of dew on the grass, for the translucent pink of a baby rabbit's ear backlit by the morning sun. I think, *This is all a gift.* Then I take it one step further, to think about my children, who are even greater gifts to be grateful for."

I often find it helpful to block off prayer time for nothing but thanks. I mentally list the things for which I am grateful: a loving wife, children who are thriving, a house that keeps us warm in winter and cool in summer, meals that keep our bodies strong, work to do, friends who care. Or as I go through the day, I try to preserve a mind of thankfulness. One morning not long ago, I decided to devote the entire day to thanksgiving. As much as I could, whenever I prayed I would not ask or seek or tell; I would only thank. On the surface it was a normal day, but deep inside I was rejoicing. I was celebrating God. As I write these words, the sunshine of a crisp October morning is streaming into my room through the window near my desk. Not only do I enjoy it, I can thank Someone for it. I thereby learn lessons in gratitude anew.

So it is not denial or flight from reality that has us expressing thanks; it is recognition that life itself is a gift. That even the hardest times contain traces of a goodness worthy of our gratefulness—if we will but look.

✦

Every now and then I ask myself how I can live with more wonder, praise, and thanksgiving. I would like not to be so forgetful of God's goodness. Brother Lawrence, who penned the spiritual classic *The Practice of the Presence of God*, spoke of keeping himself in a "simple attentiveness and a loving gaze upon God."[6] At first, as we try to live lives even faintly characterized by praise, we will find it easy to fall back into old patterns. I know that I get pulled into old patterns of stress and hurried forgetfulness. But I also sense that I can learn new habits of enjoying God. I want more to fill my thoughts with promises of God's constancy and dependability. I need to call to mind the many times he has shown his faithfulness in the hard moments of my past. Somehow I would like to immerse my praying in the praises of the Bible, the church's worship and music of faith, and the words of spiritual writers who have learned the language of adoring devotion. Then a shaft of sunlight, a starry night, a child's loving gaze point me back toward the Maker and Sustainer.

Might not life be different if enjoying God formed the backdrop of our praying and living? As we wash the dishes after supper, as we sit at our desks doing finances, as we wait with bated breath for a call from a wayward child, what if we filled our minds with what we believe about a caring, wonderful God?

PRAYERS

Worthy of praise from every mouth,
of confession from every tongue,
of worship from every creature,

is your glorious name, O Father, Son, and Holy Spirit:
who created the world in your grace
and by your compassion saved the world.
To thy majesty, O God, ten thousand times ten thousand
    bow down and adore, singing and praising without
        ceasing and saying,
Holy, holy, holy, Lord God of hosts;
Heaven and earth are full of your praises;
Hosanna in the highest.

—FROM A FIFTH-CENTURY NESTORIAN LITURGY (adapted)

We worship you, O Lord God, and give thanks to you for your
great glory and power, which you show to your servants in
your wonderful world. All the things which we enjoy are from
your mighty hand, and you alone are to be praised for all the
blessings of the life that now is. Make us thankful to you for
all your mercies and more ready to serve you with all our heart;
for the sake of Jesus Christ. Amen.

—THE NARROW WAY (1869)

NOT AFRAID TO ASK:

PETITION AND INTERCESSION

A prayer in its simplest definition is merely a
wish turned Godward.

—PHILLIPS BROOKS

More things are wrought by prayer than
this world dreams of.

—ALFRED LORD TENNYSON

Some people think God does not like to be troubled with
our constant asking. The way to trouble God is not to
come at all.

—DWIGHT L. MOODY

I have heard that sometimes our earliest memories from childhood
prefigure important themes in our lives.

In my earliest memory I am knocking on a locked bedroom door.
I must have been three or four years old. I am standing outside my
parents' bedroom, clamoring and calling to get in. On the door's
other side, my napping parents wanted only some afternoon rest. But
why should a door stand between us? Everything in me focused on
asking, on getting through.

It was that way again when I was twenty-two. I earnestly wanted my parents to come to my wedding. But their picture for me was that I would marry only in my mid- to late-twenties, certainly not before I completed grad school. They insisted that a young man should be settled in a job before he thinks about marriage. Their fears, their unwillingness to let go of their expectations and plans for me made them refuse to come to the wedding. How I asked and asked them to come! Through heated, sometimes tearful arguments, through impassioned letters, I tried to persuade. I never stopped asking. Nor did I stop wanting their blessing once I was married. Their coming around took years, and the advent of grandchildren certainly didn't hurt that process. But I also know that my asking had something to do with the outcome.

Throughout my forty-some years of life, I have found myself often assuming the posture of knocking and asking. I do it differently now, of course, than I did as a toddler. As an adult I have learned some challenging lessons about the need to wait on some answers. But in relationships, on the job, or doing much of anything that involves others, I cannot go for long without actively expressing my wants and hopes. Who of us can? In healthy relationships—especially intimate ones—we cannot stand passively by. Few things come more naturally to us than asking.

What is true for any earthly relationship also holds true for our relationship with God in prayer. We may not always ask for what we most need, of course. Our asking will sometimes reflect our agendas and whims more than God's will. But even that reality need not make us hesitate. The important thing is to turn our longings Godward. The vital thing is to weave prayer into the daily fabric of ordinary life.

"Prayer," a towering, white-haired, gravelly voiced professor from my graduate school once said, "is a form of protest with God against reality." I love that line. It slays forever the myth that spirituality makes us greet with a shrug life's status quo or the world's injustices. Prayer will not lead us to accept every circumstance with passive calm. Folding our hands in prayer is not an act of resignation. A quarrel with our world as we know it can be a great ally in the spiritual life. A desire for change often *drives* us to prayer.

Some people find this militant picture of prayer surprising. When a character in Fyodor Dostoyevsky's *The Brothers Karamazov* comes across a room of monks, he articulates a stereotype we have of people devoted to prayer: "Here in this hermitage are twenty-five saints being saved. They look at one another and eat cabbages."[1] But prayer is not simply quiet withdrawal from the world; it can represent the profoundest kind of engagement with the world. Spirituality is not a retreat to indifference. Asking—even the impetuous and noisy kind— holds a hallowed place in our talking to God because sometimes we must pray for what can be. Or pray against what is.

Remember Tevye's song in *Fiddler on the Roof*? He wondered aloud if it would really "spoil some vast eternal plan" if God would make him a rich man.[2] He asked the question with a kind of winking whimsy. But beneath his playful asking was a serious desire to enlist God in what happened in everyday life. Prayer invites God to act in the troubling arenas of life that so need his intervention. We live in a world of weapons of mass destruction, Alzheimer's disease, and molested innocents. Every day I see evidence that things around me and people next to me need help. No caring person can glibly, blithely assent to the world as it is. Nor do we need to. We can pray. We can ask.

It comes as a surprise to some to hear that the words for prayer in the original languages of the Bible literally mean "ask," "request," even "beg" and "beseech." "To the LORD I cry aloud," David the psalmist wrote (3:4). "Give ear to my words," he boldly prayed again, "consider my sighing.... In the morning I lay my requests before you and wait in expectation" (5:1,3). In the Old Testament we hear more than once a thundering cry for divine help, or an agonized "Why?" or

"How long?" Prayer is an outlet for the nagging, restless feeling that tells us all is not right.

I see this in the New Testament as well. Jesus was frank and uncondemning in acknowledging that we will often come to God with urgent requests on our lips. "Ask…," he said with blunt imperatives, "seek…knock" (Matthew 7:7). He himself came to God asking, begging God to keep his followers together, to give him guidance, and for at least a moment, to keep him from facing a horrible death.

Jesus not only modeled a frank, no-nonsense willingness to ask; he told—with perhaps a twinkle in his eye—a wonderfully odd story to make sure we don't give up on asking prayer. A woman, he said, a widow, kept nagging a crabby judge for "justice against [her] adversary." She felt wronged and would not stop pestering the judge until he ruled on her behalf. She was persistent to the point of rudeness. She had nerve. Why did the case come out in her favor? The official couldn't care less about God or widows. He responded, Jesus said, so the woman would not "eventually wear…out" the poor man with her nagging (Luke 18:1-8). Think about it: If an irritable, insensitive judge will respond, how much more will God?

Asking is not the *only* ingredient of prayer, but it is where most of us start. And it is the kind of praying the biblical greats most often unblushingly raised to God. They prayed for forgiveness for their sins, for success in their work, for many years of vigorous life. They filled their prayers with requests for their nation, for victory in war, for justice to win out, for people to turn to God, for God's kingdom to come. And so we, too, can freely, unselfconsciously ask.

❖

On this basic, almost instinctual level, asking prayer makes wonderful sense. But think about it a little more deeply, and it may not seem so simple. Questions may crowd our practice of prayer.

As C. S. Lewis mused, we say that God knows all, that nothing is hidden from his sight. Yet much of our praying seems to consist of informing him of things. Or at least reminding him. Isn't asking prayer redundant? Couldn't things be more spiritually "efficient"? God could read our minds and search our hearts.

Then there is the objection that perhaps we should assume that whatever comes is God's best. Isn't anything else interfering with the plans of Someone who already knows better than we what should happen?

A journalist friend of mine takes an even blunter view. I was talking to her about a man she had just interviewed for a book on prayer that she was writing. One person in particular bothered her. "When this guy goes jogging in the morning," she told me with exasperation, "he prays for the people living in the houses he passes." Such an approach is "prayer as magic," she said with distaste. Prayer is the encounter of the soul with God, she believes, not coming to him with a list of things needing manipulating or fixing, things God already sees and knows.

Physician and prayer researcher Larry Dossey also takes a dim view of asking prayer. He believes this kind of praying grows out of a primitive view of the universe, one in which "God is installed outside us, usually high above, as if in stationary orbit, functioning as a sort of master communications satellite.... We 'send' our prayers 'upward' to God, who may or may not choose to function as a relay station to the object of our prayer."[3] In other words, we should outgrow such uncultured conceptions of a God who answers requests. Praying must move beyond expecting (or asking for) definite outcomes. Only grade-school piety "tells God what to do."

It is true enough that we are sometimes tempted to use prayer as a kind of magic wand. We want growth without cost, results without effort, answers without the soul-searching work of asking. Sometimes our requests resemble panicked cries for a quick God-fix.

But such objections do not negate the place of proper asking. Not if God willingly has chosen to act through us and through our asking.

Not if God wants to enlist us in his plans and chooses to invite us to participate through prayer. Of course, he is powerful enough not to have to call on our puny muscle and stuttering prayers. Yes, he already knows what we tell him. But for our sakes and for the sake of others, he becomes the Great Delegator. He allows us to participate with him in what is and what is to come.

C. S. Lewis articulated the struggle to grasp such an exalted view of prayer in this way, picturing a conversation with a wise friend who helps him with his objections:

> "Praying for specific things," said I, "always seems like advising God how to run the world. Wouldn't it be better to assume that he knows best?" "On the same principle," said [my friend], "I suppose you never ask the man next to you to pass the salt, because God knows best whether you ought to have salt or not. And I suppose you never take an umbrella because God knows best whether you ought to be wet or dry." "That's quite different," I protested. "I don't see why," said he. "The odd thing is that He should let us influence the course of events at all. But since he lets us do it in one way, I don't see why he shouldn't let us do it in another."[4]

God fiercely defends our right to participate with him in the way things turn out. He most certainly rules as a Sovereign Lord in charge of the universe he has made. But God does not manipulate like a marionette master all that happens. He absorbs our eager longings into his purposes and holy creativity. He puts the exercise of his power at least faintly at our disposal. God listens, moves, and acts as we pray. As E. M. Bounds, a deeply thoughtful twentieth-century writer on prayer put it, "Only God can move mountains. But faith and prayer move God."

Perhaps this truth can best be fleshed out in an ancient story. Picture a halting, tongue-tied ancient Hebrew leader named Moses. He quakes when he senses that God is near. His knees knock. He stutters.

But look at him, arguing with God! While Moses confers with God on Mount Sinai and receives the Ten Commandments, the people in the valley melt their gold to fashion an idol. God seems almost unable to believe it. "I have seen these people," he tells Moses as Moses is about to head back down the mountain, "and they are a stiff-necked people. Now leave me alone so that my anger may burn against them...."

"But Moses sought the favor of the LORD his God," we read. Here is what he prayed:

> O LORD,...why should your anger burn against your people,
> whom you brought out of Egypt with great power and a
> mighty hand? ...Turn from your fierce anger; relent and do
> not bring disaster on your people.

Then a remarkable conclusion: "The LORD relented and did not bring on his people the disaster he had threatened" (Exodus 32:9-12,14).

Such a picture may boggle the imagination. It seems hard to believe that God looks to us to do things and to pray toward ends he *could* accomplish by fiat and thunderclap. Certainly, when God wills something, he will bring it to pass as he intends, but that does not exclude our asking. Perhaps God both intends for some particular thing to happen *and* wants to use us to make it happen. Perhaps with some things he wants and plans to do, he even *waits* for our prayers before he releases his full activity or blessing. In so many ways, he seems to work through the slow, the steady, the *human*. In prayer we take hold of his willingness to listen to our requests and move; we exercise our right as children to influence a loving parent.

And such a view confers on us responsibility. It means that God uses our offerings—our meager check written to help feed the hungry, our quiet smile of encouragement, and, no less, our praying—to transfigure the world and unfold unimaginable purposes. Jesus tells us not only to ask, seek, and knock, but he says that if we do, we will receive, we will find, and a door will open. This points not only to a promise of what *can* happen; it suggests what may *not* happen if we ignore the invitation. The world does not bow to an impersonal fate. God is on the move, and he enlists us in his kingdom advance.

This has been a great and freeing insight to me. I grew up in a Christian denomination that tends to downplay the role of the supernatural in God's dealing with humankind. I often heard the maxim, "Prayer doesn't change things; it changes *us*." And who can argue with the conviction that prayer can and should transform us? But these words were often said as though personal transformation is *all* prayer accomplishes. It was almost the idea, as one popular spirituality book suggests, that prayer is "just talking to" yourself and "reprogramming" your internal computer.[5]

When I enrolled in a hospital chaplaincy apprenticeship program during seminary, the subject of praying for patients came up in our training group. "I pray out loud with a patient when he or she asks for it," my chaplaincy supervisor told us. "The patient often finds it emotionally therapeutic." For him, that was about it. It made patients feel better. But for him it seemed to do nothing to influence God or shape the outcome of events. It would never fall on responsive ears.

But we can say more than that prayer reassures us when we are needy. Much more. God stands in relation to the world and its events not as an autocrat but as an artist whose work of art shows in every stroke or chip the contribution of an apprentice.[6] "The strongest one in Christ's kingdom," wrote E. M. Bounds, "is he who can knock the best."[7]

God listens attentively to our asking, not because he is cowed by us or our demands, but because he *chooses* to do so. Prayer changes things not because it is a magical formula but because behind it is nothing less than the Creator's power. Prayer moves the hand that holds the universe. There is more to our asking than we can ever imagine because there is more to God than we can ever fathom. And there is in him a generosity that exceeds our imaginations.

Why does God choose to give us, through our praying, a role in what happens? There is still mystery here, a reality not settled by philosophical or theological reasoning alone. Ultimately, the best answer must be the language of relationship.

I ask things of my wife—to hold me when I'm needy, to hear me confess my hidden insecurities—that I would never ask of a stranger or my next-door neighbor. If I never turned to her for what only she can give me, she would know something was gravely wrong. Asking often points to the deepest intimacy.

Is it so very different with God? Why do we so fear that we will insult God by our requests? Asking demonstrates that we need him. That we believe he can help us. Such prayers are born of trust. They point to our hope that our lives are held in the arms of a personal Presence, not caught in the random processes of impersonal events. God chooses to use our praying because asking always puts us in touch with him.

⁘⬦⁘

Another conviction that helps us understand the importance of asking prayer: On the other side of our asking is God's answering.

When talking about asking prayer, Jesus directed our eyes to a caring parent: "Which of you, if his son asks for bread, will give him a stone? Or if he asks for a fish, will give him a snake? If you, then, though you are evil, know how to give good gifts to your children, how much more will your Father in heaven give good gifts to those who ask him!" (Matthew 7:9-11). I respond when my children ask me for help on school projects, bring me wish lists for their birthdays, or reach out for bedtime hugs. I may not always deem their requests possible or advisable to grant. I won't always give them what they request. I don't make their asking the *only* guidance or criterion for how I respond. But I do allow and even welcome their asking. I expect it.

While working on this book, a friend of mine phoned to tell me that his wife no longer has cancer, even though she was diagnosed years ago with a grave, pernicious form of the disease. She could well have not survived. I reminded my friend that at my church we have included her name Sunday after Sunday in the "Prayers of the People." Sunday after Sunday she has been remembered by hundreds of people. Can I say that those prayers are the sole reason for her healing? I cannot. But still I believe that God used our asking. And who knows in what powerful ways our constancy and persistence made the difference?

Ask my friend Charlene Baumbich, a writer, speaker, and housewife, if she has had any recent memorable experiences of asking prayer, and she will tell you of a summer day that had dawned hot, humid, and oppressive. It was a great day to stay in air-conditioned comfort, especially for someone with her history of passing out on blistering days. But she had volunteered through the Kiwanis Club to chaperon some physically challenged children on a trip to the local zoo. "Here I was," she told me, "supposed to be pushing a wheelchair, and they were going to need one for me." As she was getting ready to leave home, she called to ask a couple of friends to pray for her stamina. And she prayed for herself. She *asked.*

When she arrived at the group's meeting place, she discovered that one child's mom had decided at the last minute to accompany her child on the outing. Suddenly there was no need for Charlene to go. "I believe," she told me, "that God moved that other mother to go along. He answered my prayer better than I would have dared ask. And perhaps he was answering that mother's prayer for a chance to get out of the house, for time to bond with her child. I asked and he answered."

We hold such requests lightly sometimes, especially when they concern our own comfort. But is there any reason not to ask? Asking only becomes magic, I believe, when we try to wield prayer apart from an intimate relationship with God. It is no talisman, no Aladdin's lamp to rub, no formula hatched in the dark womb of magical arts. When we seek the gifts apart from the hand of the Giver, when we ask only to gain advantage, when we ignore the face of the One to whom we turn, then something has gone awry. Then we ask wrongly. But the sin is not in asking but in trying to use God apart from loving him.

❖

There is another way in which asking is crucial. And it is best illustrated by something that happened to me a few years ago.

One morning I awoke filled with stress, anxious about deadlines at the office where I was working at the time. The night before, my wife commented on how distant and self-absorbed I had seemed throughout the evening. Even my praying that morning focused on what I needed to get done, what I was feeling, the fears I was nursing. But then, as I kept praying, I began remembering the many people I wanted to pray for. I prayed for my wife. I lifted up my children by name. I prayed for my then-living mother's need to know that God was near. I remembered a relative who was struggling with doubt and disbelief. I even prayed for my co-workers and the company we work for. Before I knew it, I found my prayers taking me out of myself. I became aware of a wider world around me. Asking pulled me out of my self-absorption.

While asking prayer may include petition, in which we pray for ourselves and run the gamut from asking for a new, more reliable car or a more satisfying job to asking God to make us more faithful, it also supremely includes intercession, in which we pray for others. Our word *intercession* comes from the Latin *inter*, which means "between," and *cedere*, which means "to go." To intercede is to go between two persons in the hope of reconciling differences or to plead with someone on another's behalf. In the context of prayer, it means making sure we bring others into our times of conversation with God.

The "how" of asking in intercessory prayer can be quite simple. Many people who appear in my prayers are only vaguely identified. I may not even know the name of someone I pray for, as when I pass an interstate accident and breathe a prayer for "that person laying on the roadside beside a wrecked car." Perhaps I will pray for "the African refugee I saw on the news tonight." I need not wax eloquent.

Ellis Peters, in her medieval whodunit *A Morbid Taste for Bones,* paints the following scene of a monk's simple asking prayer: "He prayed as he breathed, forming no words and making no specific requests, only holding in his heart, like broken birds in cupped hands, all those people who were in stress or grief."[8] One friend of mine depends on God to help him form his intercessions. He sits quietly, meditatively, until God gently brings to his mind those persons or situations that need prayer. I once read of a woman confined to a bed who kept a "family album" of some two hundred photographs of friends, missionaries, and others she wanted to pray for. She worked her way through the entire album each week, praying over the pictures. I have a friend who jogs her memory to pray for people undergoing surgery or some trial by writing down the date and time of the event in her Day-Timer calendar. That way she is sure to pray for the person at the actual hour or moment of need.

I find I can pray for people whenever I think of them, wherever I am. Simple, stabbed, flash prayers of "Help so-and-so" or "Be with my neighbor right now" are, the Bible seems to assure us, welcomed by God.

I also try to do more than offer occasional or random prayers. Because of the truth of the Chinese proverb that says the finest mind is less reliable than the simplest ink, I do best if I do not always leave my petitions and intercessions to memory. I try to keep a list of prayer concerns, and as nearly as I can come to it, I sit down with it daily. At any given time I have a couple dozen names and concerns to review. Every so often I cross off the list an answered prayer or an issue that has passed and start over with a new list every few months. (Some names—those of the people I'm closest to—stay on the list season after season.) I pray for people at my church, I pray for my work, I pray for more patience, I pray for greater love for God—and I pray for this book! But most often I feel called to remember in prayer the people who crowd into my life.

I try to do more than rush through a recital of people's names. Too often, I confess, I don't do much more than that. But while I like to pause and articulate the obvious need, I also try to go deeper, to uncover new layers of what the person I know or care about must be experiencing. I especially try to pray graciously for those who have hurt or angered me. One friend of mine likes to say, "Take the things you see in people that annoy you and turn them into prayer. God shows you sin and brokenness in people not so you can criticize and judge them, but so that you can pray for them." .

I also try to pray with a global perspective. Starving masses, wars in far-flung countries, even moral decline in this country, all find a place in my prayers. The New Testament urges "that requests, prayers, intercession and thanksgiving be made for everyone—for kings and all those in authority, that we may live peaceful and quiet lives" (1 Timothy 2:1-2).

Can I measure the impact of my praying compared with the juggernaut of world violence? the pernicious power of infectious disease? the pervasiveness of poverty? No. But who knows how God uses it? Perhaps the prayers of his people are, in Frank Laubach's memorable image, like the stones filling a swamp which, one by one, hundred by hundred, seem to do little good, until at last a stone appears on the surface and the swamp disappears.

How does such praying "work"? Not as a function of some impersonal force "activated" by our asking. And, just as clearly, prayer's influence does not ignore human choice. Some suggest that perhaps our prayers for another person mostly lower the threshold of the prayed-for's own openness to God or to a new set of circumstances. They may serve to unlock a gate, but they do not coerce. God's response to our prayers does not violate a person's ability to choose. Herein, once again, we peer at mystery. Yet, I believe, in our prayers lies great power, the power of the God who invites us to pray in the first place because he wants to use our asking.

⊹⊰◈⊱⊹

Asking makes spiritual sense in another way. It saturates our lives with a sense of possibility. "Humankind stands at a crossroads," someone once said, tongue firmly in cheek. "One way leads to despair and hopelessness. The other to total destruction. Pray that we have the wisdom to choose correctly."

Prayer reminds us that we need never despair. The One to whom we appeal is a God of justice and power and love. He does not wipe out evil with one fell swoop—at least, he has not chosen to yet. But in prayer we participate as hopeful subversives against the power of darkness and evil. The Bible speaks often of a coming kingdom of God that is here now in part and is advancing through God's exercise.

When your daughter has run away, your job has been stolen out from under you, your relationship with God has gone dry and barren, or a little boy is hounded and hurt because of the color of his skin, praying reminds us that all is not hopeless. It reminds us that even when we feel powerless, we can turn to Someone who is able to do immeasurably beyond our ability to think and even imagine.

⊹⊰◈⊱⊹

One Saturday morning my wife and I lingered over breakfast, reading the morning newspaper. As Jill flipped through the local-news section, an ad caught her eye. A church was announcing its pastor's message for the following morning's worship service. The title was intriguing: "Don't Be Afraid to Ask."

I don't know what the sermon was about, but what struck me

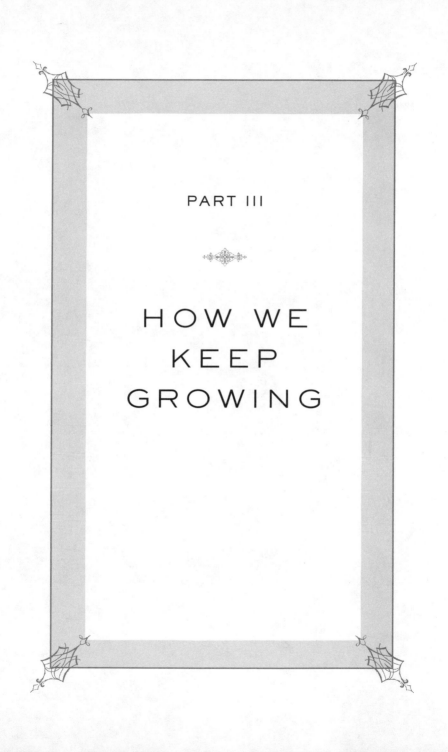

PART III

HOW WE KEEP GROWING

EMOTIONS AND GETTING

REAL WITH GOD

I have risen against His justice, protested His silence and sometimes His absence, but my anger rises up within faith and not outside it.

—ELIE WIESEL, *All Rivers Run to the Sea*

The Prayer of Complaint...has been largely lost in our modern, sanitized religion, but the Bible abounds with it.

—RICHARD FOSTER, *Prayer*

From the beginning of our romance, my wife and I have easily expressed tender feelings to each other. Sometimes we animatedly discuss the details of our jobs and family; other times we expose corners of our deeper selves. But by far our toughest times of communicating are when one of us is angry. Early in our courtship was the hardest of all. When incensed, Jill would sometimes walk away—literally. My strategy looked more mannered but was just as destructive: I would go inside myself, clam up. Jill and I had to learn to argue. We needed lessons in how to be angry without withdrawing. We had to find ways to channel our fuming or offended feelings.

I believe something similar takes place in prayer. When we get angry with God for something we think he could have helped us avoid, we are tempted to walk away or pull back. We are not sure our churning emotions belong in the presence of God. We become reserved and, often, are not too motivated to pray.

I believe our emotions—all of them—belong in our prayers. "If we are without human feelings," wrote Thomas Merton, "we cannot love God in the way in which we are meant to love him—as [human beings]."[1] Our prayers represent not just what we say but who we are, with all our complex longings and feelings. To be close to someone, even when that Someone is God, will inevitably run us through a gamut of emotion. To think that prayer should be a monotone patter is to rob it of its power. To read the Psalms or other devotional outpourings of pray-ers, classical and contemporary, is to witness a dazzling emotional tapestry. A wide and sometimes wild range of feelings accompany a walk with God.

So we can be real with God. And since most of us already know that we can exult with adoration or bow our heads in contrition or intently, urgently ask, this chapter will not focus on the expected sentiments. I want to look at what troubles us more: our occasional sense of disappointment with God, even the anger that sometimes makes us stew or smolder or turn away from him.

The subject is not merely academic for me. Some years ago, when my wife and I had moved to Houston to start a new church and things weren't happening as we had hoped, I often felt trapped by expectations—mine, those of church members, and those of the people who commissioned us to go. Although I believed God had led us to Houston, he didn't seem all that interested in making things "work." This is what I wrote in my journal one morning:

> I awoke feeling mad at God. I didn't want to pray or read
> Scripture. I saw my Scripture memory verses by the bedside,
> and an image of my stomach turning flashed through my
> mind. I thought of praying several times during the day, but

recoiled at the idea. My anger—or desire to keep God at a distance—seems to paralyze me.

Our first reaction may be to shrink from such feelings. They seem very "unprayerful." But we do better to admit and acknowledge them, not submerge them. We can consider later where they should take us. For now, we are the wiser if we bring them out into view. "Do not let it be imagined," noted Paul Tournier, "that one must remain silent about one's feelings of rebellion in order to enter into dialogue with God. Quite the opposite is the truth: it is precisely when one expresses them that a dialogue of truth begins."[2]

Someone once wrote to me of how she managed to include even painful, angry emotion in prayer:

> I went through a nightmare of emotions, from sorrow and despair to frustration and rage. My "prayer life" as I was used to it became nonexistent. I found I could *not* pray—not in the way I believed prayer had to be done. Oh, I could "pray" the psalms—I was living the psalms! But all other prayer became dry, impossible. What I found myself doing throughout that long summer was questioning—my faith, my God, my purpose for being. I found myself one night absolutely ranting and raging at God, asking him…no, *telling* him what I thought of the whole situation. I demanded that he show himself to me.
>
> I was horrified with myself the next day, wondering if I had committed a sin by being so "truthful." But a good friend pointed out to me that my ranting was probably the closest I had come in a long time to true prayer.

Much in Christian tradition—such as the Psalms, with their frequent outbursts of anger against enemies, and the prophets, with their plaintive, impatient questioning of God—recognizes, as we often fail to do, the pervasiveness of anger. Our biblical mentors respected strong, fiery emotions. They did not try to deny them.

"I never found a blissful peace to disappear into," my friend remembered of her angry praying. "My life continued to be a challenging disarray of routine, of insecurity, of emotion. But I found that I was sustained in many ways by God's grace—not in any concrete way that can be categorized, but things 'happened,' good things that might have only been coincidences except I believe there are no coincidences with God." Had she "broken through" that night she ranted? Had her acknowledgment of what she felt let her once again approach God instead of avoiding him?

⋯⦿⋯

But we worry. Wouldn't we be offending a righteous, holy God if we rail at him? Some, recalling Jesus's words about the "blasphemy against the [Holy] Spirit" (Matthew 12:31), fear that yelling at God is the "unforgivable sin."

That particular fear is easily set to rest. The "blasphemy" against the Holy Spirit that troubles some people's consciences is not railing at God. It refers rather to those in Jesus's own day who rejected the Spirit's work in Jesus and his ministry, even though they should have known better. It has to do with icy *unbelief,* not hot anger. It has to do not so much with what we say as with our basic disposition toward God. To blaspheme is to utterly reject, not to howl in pain.

Indeed, anger is often the first sign that we care about something or someone. Just as a couple's constructive anger need not detonate their marriage, so also is our impatience with God hardly enough to send him running. He does not ask us to walk on eggshells around him. He is a jealous God, as the Bible says, but not oversensitive. So, as my friend Charlene Baumbich tells me, "Box, fight, scream, holler, cry, give thanks and praise. Tell God everything that's on your mind, because he knows anyway."

God would rather have us come to him angry than not come at all. For then, at least, we are angry in his presence rather than pushing him away in our frustration. Better angry than distant. Emotion, even strong negative emotion, keeps us in contact with God.

And sometimes, letting something boil over rather than letting it steam and simmer gets us through a difficult time more cleanly. The petulant anger of my Texas journal entry was short-lived; had I never written it down, it would be lost from memory. Yet could it be that my writing it down and expressing my anger helped me not be troubled by it for long?

Anger with God, I believe, is not the same as abandoning God. Whole sections of the Psalms are crowded with complaint and lament. And yet note: They always find expression as *prayers*. The protest is couched, as concentration-camp survivor Elie Wiesel wrote,[3] in the name of faith in God:

> But I cry to you for help, O LORD;
>   in the morning my prayer comes before you.
> Why, O LORD, do you reject me
>   and hide your face from me? (Psalm 88:13-14)

Such prayers poignantly express the psalmist's hurt and pathos. As does this psalm:

> My God, my God, why have you forsaken me?
>   Why are you so far from saving me,
>   so far from the words of my groaning?

> O my God, I cry out by day, but you do not answer,
>   by night, and am not silent. (Psalm 22:1-2)

But the indignant words are *addressed to God.* The moaning is sand-wiched between the speaking of God's name. The context is the God to whom we turn in our hurt: "O God, *whom I praise,* do not remain silent" (Psalm 109:1, emphasis added).

These psalms, and other prayers like them, writes Richard Foster, "teach us to pray our inner conflicts and contradictions. They allow us to shout out our forsakenness in the dark caverns of abandonment and then hear the echo return to us over and over until we...recant of them, only to shout them out again. They give us permission to shake our fist at God one moment and break into [praise] again the next."[4]

And they teach us that anger usually gives way to praise. It is hard to be sullen for long when addressing a good God.

❧

A friend experienced significant disappointment with childbearing. For years she was infertile. Finally, she conceived and delivered two healthy children, but then she miscarried twice within six months. Adding to Karen's grief, the doctor told her she should not have any more children. "I felt God was saying 'I want good things for you' at the same time he was letting awful things happen to me."

Finally, she told me,

> I lost hope. I started asking, "Why do I believe in God? *Is*
> there a God?" A Christian friend came to visit me in the
> hospital to talk and pray with me. While he talked I thought,
> *I don't believe a word you are saying.* I felt no one understood
> the pain I was in. Then I began to think about my life before
> I knew God, and I realized that to go back to my "pagan" life
> would lead to even greater despair.

Finally, in desperation I cried out to God, "I'm in pain. I'm angry at you. But out of faith I will follow you."

At that point I sensed a Presence in the room unlike any I had ever sensed. Then I glimpsed a mental picture of the Lord in the room with me. In the vision, I was on the floor in a puddle of pain. But the Lord put his arms around me in a strong embrace. He lifted me to my feet. He began to dance with me.

Karen allowed her anger to turn her to God. Once she got near him, the picture changed. She came through to the other side.

That is how it happens in the Psalms. The cries and protests come out of faith, so they lead back to faith. One moment the pray-er is crying out in forsakenness: "You do not answer." The next he is affirming the trustworthiness of God:

> *Yet* you are enthroned as the Holy One;
>> you are the praise of Israel.
> In you our fathers put their trust;
>> they trusted and you delivered them.
> They cried to you and were saved;
>> in you they trusted and were not disappointed.
>> (Psalm 22:3-5, emphasis added)

I like the story of how a journalist made a discovery similar to the psalmist's.

While on a photojournalism assignment in Virginia early on a June morning in 1984, Frank Bianco learned that Michael, one of his two sons, was killed in a collision. Already wavering in his religious faith, Frank responded to the tragedy by bitterly blaming God.

Almost immediately, Bianco also experienced a cruel twist of the grieving process: He had developed a bizarre amnesia when it came to Michael. All memories of his son vanished. But when a writing assignment took him to a monastery, something else happened:

When I entered [the monastery's church], about fifty white-
and black-robed monks were already in their choir stalls
directly below. Five minutes later, they were standing, facing
forward, when a knock signaled them to begin.

I do not recall particular words or phrases from the liturgy
that followed. I know I was struck by the monks' genuine reverence. They were not mouthing rituals. They were singing carefully, slowly, as one disciplined voice. They were talking to
someone. I did not doubt that any more than I would doubt the
presence of a catcher if I were watching a pitcher winding up.

I glanced around the church, looking for that catcher. But
the tabernacle was not glowing. Nor was the crucifix over the
altar moving. And the light streaming through the stained-
glass windows did not alter a bit. No, everything was perfectly
normal. With one exception. For the first time since he had
died, memories of Michael began to flood my mind.[5]

Whenever Bianco returned to a church or monastery, the memories flooded back. Once outside the building, the memories vanished
again.

But still Bianco raged at God. One day, after pouring out his grief
and anger while he stood in a worship service, Bianco realized, "The
God I had reviled and rejected had been waiting to mourn with me,
burned with sorrow he would share with me.… God had never given
up on me.… I heard the words, 'I know, I know. As you did, as you
still do, I love him too. I know.'"

That was the turning point in Bianco's anger. He discovered that
God hurt with him. "I stayed [in the church]," Bianco concluded,
"weeping, as the pain poured out. But not alone. Not unconsoled.
This time I wept in the arms of my God, whom I finally allowed to
hold me in that monastery church."[6]

❖

Ultimately, prayer is an expression of who we *are*. And how we pray is part of a complex of emotions, outlooks, experiences, and psychological patterns. Even when we think we are suppressing what is going on underneath, who we are and what we are feeling and thinking affects what happens. If we stay with our anger instead of running from it, it will lead us into an intimacy with God deeper than we have ever known.

Not long after Jill and I became engaged, we fought over something. I vividly remember sitting with her on a park bench in the Princeton, New Jersey, sunshine. She was fingering her diamond engagement ring, and I expected her to hand it back to me any minute. I don't recall many of the specifics of our argument, just that it had to do with the normal stresses of joining two very separate lives and that the emotions were intense. But something kept us at it. Through shedding many tears and letting down our guard and sharing our honest frustrations, our relationship avoided meltdown. We decided we liked each other again. We realized how deep our love ran. In our talking through our anger, we saw that what drove us apart could not quench our commitment. We got up from the bench and started walking together. We have kept going ever since.

I'm glad that, angry words and all, we came out on the other side. And our relationship, even with occasional tiffs, continues to weather the challenges—as a strong marriage can. As prayer can.

PRAYERS

Lord, you know the swirl of emotions within me.
   Help me not let my anger or disappointment drive me away
     from you.
   Help me to be honest and yet not get stuck in my frustration.
Amen.

Why, O LORD, do you stand far off?
    Why do you hide yourself in times of trouble?…
Arise, LORD! Lift up your hand, O God.
    Do not forget the helpless….
You hear, O LORD, the desire of the afflicted;
    you encourage them, and you listen to their cry.

—PSALM 10:1,12,17

LISTENING FOR GOD

The moment you wake up each morning...all your wishes
and hopes for the day rush at you like wild animals. And
the first job each morning consists in shoving them all
back; in listening to that other voice, taking that other
point of view, letting that other, larger, stronger, quieter
life come flowing in.

—C. S. LEWIS, *Mere Christianity*

A man prayed, and at first he thought that prayer was talking. But he became more and more quiet until in the end
he realized that prayer is listening.

—SØREN KIERKEGAARD

An inner, secret turning to God can be made fairly steady,
after weeks and months and years of practice and lapses
and failures and returns.

—THOMAS KELLY, *A Testament of Devotion*

Not long ago I was driving to work, praying about the day ahead.
I included in my mental list the phone calls I needed to return,
a child sick at home, and my concerns about a project that had a tight
deadline. I suddenly realized how much my praying was filled with
items on my day's agenda. I realized how little time I spend simply

listening to God. I felt moved to stop talking. For the rest of my trip, I made myself—my heart and my ears—available to God. What a significant shift! I received no dazzling insight. But I suddenly felt as though I was tuned in to God, not just bending his ear.

I know people, though, who are wary of listening prayer, who believe God would never deign to speak to humankind, except perhaps to near saints. I know others who greet the very idea with skepticism, who think hearing from God is akin to contact with extraterrestrials and that those who make such claims should perhaps be escorted to places where helpers wear white coats and prescribe strong medication. Still others think "mature" believers do not expect guidance for daily choices, that God sets us on earth to do our work without a childlike need for help in choosing. The idea of listening to God makes no sense to such people, not if prayer is the pouring out of our hearts and souls to God. And not if God will not communicate with us anyway.

During the "God is dead" movement of the sixties and seventies, evangelist Billy Graham once said he was sure God existed because he had talked to him that morning. "Ah, but that is not the issue," one theologian countered. "The question is, Did God talk back?"

The hesitations have some merit, of course. Who doesn't know of terrible things done in the name of "God told me to..."? People have credited (or blamed) God for actions that range from the outlandish to the pernicious. And for many choices in life, we do not need special divine guidance. We simply do our work, live as faithfully as we know how, and recognize our need to live without constantly second-guessing the opportunities or challenges that open before us.

But if God is not a mute deity, why wouldn't he speak? If he is wondrously personal, why should our praying be a monologue? And "why is it," asks comedienne Lily Tomlin, "that when we speak to God we are said to be praying, but when God speaks to us we are said to be schizophrenic?"[1] Why would God not sometimes grace us with insight that extends beyond our finite range of vision? Yes, people get the message garbled or the vision skewed. But that does not mean

God does not communicate. Through angels, miracles, a still small voice, the murmurs of conscience, and especially his written revelation in Scripture, God does not keep silent. This means that prayer must entail more than our talking. It must also include our listening.

So how do we do it?

We Listen Prayerfully to Our Lives

If God is present in the world, he is surely present in what happens to us. He unfolds his will for us in life's little moments, its turns and detours, its bright moments and dark ones. Daily events (and non-events) are a kind of alphabet through which God communicates, as Frederick Buechner reminds us in *The Alphabet of Grace*.[2] We get a job offer out of the blue that changes our career direction. Somebody tells us something we don't want to hear but need to. A parent or sibling we thought had written us off calls and struggles to say the words, "I'm proud of you." We piece together the "letters," Buechner suggests, and a kind of word forms, and suddenly we see something we might have missed.

So we pray not only for what we want to see happen; we pray about what actually does happen. We attend to our lives as they are, as they already have been. We "read life backwards" for clues about where we should go. We try to see what God is saying. We recognize that we can learn much simply by listening to what transpires around and within us.

I find that keeping a journal is one of the best ways to listen to what God might be trying to tell me through the happenings of daily life. Journaling is not so much recording the day's or week's minutiae as much as it is setting them down in light of my relationship with God. It is a prayerful discipline for me. It allows me to reflect on my ordinary experiences. I don't write every day, not by any stretch, but I do try to write a page or two every so often. Then every few months I flip back to earlier entries, and I am reminded of a promise God gave me or a new direction I sensed opening up or a friend's encouraging words. When I find themes being repeated over the years, I recognize patterns that give me direction, remind me where I'm going.

Journaling, of course, is not the only way to listen to our lives. Simply being more reflective, more alert, can help us read the clues. Especially when it comes to life's tougher moments. We learn the fine art of paying attention to a larger Voice amid all the sounds and movements.

We Learn to Listen Through Pain

We sometimes see suffering as an interruption or distraction. It even drives us to question God's existence. But there is another view.

Madeleine L'Engle, renowned author, lived through the slow, agonizing death of her husband. She found lines of poetry from William Yeats and copied them down, including the following couplet:

> But Love has pitched his mansion in
> The place of excrement.[3]

"This summer," L'Engle reflected in her journal, "is not the first time I have walked through the place of excrement and found love's mansion there. Indeed, we are more likely to find it in the place of excrement than in the sterile places. God comes where there is pain and brokenness."[4] Dark and dingy places may become the places we most clearly search for and recognize God's subtly shining light.

When we hurt, we may for the first time open our ears and our hearts. Pain wakes us up. "God whispers to us in our pleasures," said C. S. Lewis, "speaks in our consciences, but shouts in our pain: it is his megaphone to rouse a deaf world."[5] I wish it weren't so, but it is often disappointment or panic that drives me to my knees. Suffering opens us to hearing what, in our stiffness and pride and self-sufficiency, we would otherwise never bother with.

I once heard of a minister who said he had mixed feelings about praying for the physical healing of his church members' ailments because the illnesses were so good for their souls. I most definitely pray for healing for those entrusted to my pastoral care, but I understand the minister's sentiment. Many people finally slow down enough to listen only when they're flat on their backs in bed. Or only when the pain inside makes them ask some deeper questions. Our hurts often lead us to God. They bring us to moments of healthy questioning. I don't like to admit it, but sometimes struggle is the only thing that will turn me to God in dependence.

We Learn to Listen by Asking for Guidance

One of the most significant and profound ways to begin our prayer times is to tell God that we are listening. That we are ready for him to speak. I have always been moved by young Samuel in the Bible. His guardian, the temple priest Eli, coached the boy on listening: "If [God] calls you, say, 'Speak, LORD, for your servant is listening'" (1 Samuel 3:9).

When my life lacks a clear focus, or I need guidance, or I simply want to be more open to God, I find it helpful to remember this story. I go through the day quietly repeating Samuel's prayer: "Speak, Lord, for your servant is listening." Somehow this attitude and posture prepares my heart for the moment God finally does speak. God may not tell me everything I wish to know, but he is able to tell me more than if I am not alert and attuned to him.

When I pray in this way, I will often find the answer on an impending decision growing more certain. A sense of "rightness" will emerge. I don't get it right every time, of course, but something inside me says, "Yes, this is God's best." Or I will suddenly be prompted to pray for someone, only to find out later that the individual was at that moment experiencing crisis and desperately needed prayer support. If I am open, God can influence me, whether visibly or unobtrusively.

I also believe that God may influence us and speak without our knowing it. I notice a gentle restraint in much of God's communicating with us. He seems to favor the quiet and unobtrusive. We sometimes think celestial fireworks and "big" miracles make for surer signs. But God is communicating all the time. Angel messages, blinding lights, and roadside burning bushes are usually not his preferred modes. God's speaking may be no more dramatic than a gentle reminder that I am being held and watched through every circumstance.

And when the Lord does speak, it is often in a simple phrase. Some time ago I went for a morning run. I spent close to an hour praying, mostly pouring out my soul about my job, which, at that particularly busy time, had threatened to dominate my every waking moment. Finally, I felt it was time to cease my speaking and simply listen. The message that came was direct: "Your job is too important to you." But it was wonderfully freeing. It was no different from what my wife had been saying to me, but somehow hearing it from the Lord allowed me to give the message more weight. I began to see how my immersion in work came from a hankering after approval from others, not from wanting to love and serve God.

One woman tells of a terrible time of crisis. She spent many hours in anxiety. But she also prayed. Then, she remembers,

> One morning, in a half-asleep, half-awake state, I kept hearing three musical notes in my head [that made me feel] very calm and peaceful. I finally awakened fully and while dressing realized that the tune in my head was a song I had sung in choir when I was in high school twenty years earlier. The words that accompany those three notes are "Trust in God"... I took it as a message, and though the crisis [my husband and I] were in did not change for another seven months, I was never as fearful or worried again. When the crisis ended, the outcome was much better than I ever dreamed possible.[6]

Of course, God may not say anything in particular when we listen for him. We may hear no celestial sound bite. In an interview with Mother Teresa of Calcutta, Dan Rather asked, "What do you say to

God when you pray?" Mother Teresa looked at him with her dark, soulful eyes and said quietly, "I listen." Slightly flustered, Rather tried again. "Well, then, what does God say?" Mother Teresa smiled. "He listens."[7] Profound communication can often take place in the subtlest of ways, through a still small voice. Or loving silence.

We Listen by Paying Attention to Revealed Truth

Much of listening is simply absorbing the truth and presence of God already made evident. Especially at the beginning, when we are learning how to discern God's voice, we need not place heavy expectations upon ourselves. We relax and don't worry too much about abundant revelations.

Fortunately we are not left to our own devices when it comes to understanding what is true. One of the primary ways God speaks is through the recorded revelations of the prophets and sages and apostles of Scripture. "All Scripture," Paul the apostle reminds us, "is God-breathed and is useful for teaching, rebuking, correcting and training in righteousness" (2 Timothy 3:16). God also speaks through the wisdom of history's great spiritual teachers. And I believe God speaks most clearly through the life, death, and resurrection of Jesus—the Word made flesh, as the Bible calls him. Much of my prayer for guidance leads me to him. And begins there. Much of listening is taking to heart what I already know or what God has already given in his revelation through Christ.

For in spite of our culture's penchant for rugged individualism and frontier independence, there is much we cannot calculate and find on our own. The goal of life is not ingenuity or spiritual inventiveness. It is to let our thoughts be molded by revealed reality. We cannot philosophize our way to truth. When we try, we end up confounded and befuddled—or just plain wrong. Instead, we soak ourselves in the wisdom of Scripture. We listen to what God tells us through his written Word, the Bible, and the Living Word, Jesus, in whom, says the apostle Paul, "all the fullness of the Deity lives in bodily form" (Colossians 2:9). And, Paul goes on to say, "you have been given fullness in Christ" (verse 10), which means we stay open to the guidance of God's spirit, who helps us live "in" Christ.

I was intrigued to find that behind our word *absurd* lies the Latin root *surdus,* which means "deaf." In our deafness, in our occasional reluctance to open to truth outside ourselves, our lives become absurd. By way of contrast, I learned that the word *obedient* comes from a Latin word for "listening." We move from absurdity to obedience, from floundering confusion to conformity to God's will, through listening.

It's important that our listening be more than sentimentality. Counterfeits are sometimes mistaken for authentic spirituality. Both can make us mist up and feel warm inside. And our hearts are deviously clever in helping us justify and rationalize what we want. To be undiscerning and unguided in spirituality would be like going for a walk in the forest, someone has said, picking and eating every mushroom or root we see. For all their resemblance to edible varieties, some of the forest's attractions can poison us. Likewise, spiritual look-alikes not grounded in the tested truth of Scripture can make our souls sick, sometimes fatally.

This is where Scripture can guide. God "chose to give us birth through the word of truth" (James 1:18). We don't stand under the stars and let our ruminations guide us to God, as some New Age spiritual writers seem to suggest we do. We read. We listen. We are taught. We let our words be formed by the words others used before us. And we spend time getting to know the One whom we address. That often happens no more thoroughly than through absorbing what he has already told us about himself through the Bible.

I try to ensure, then, that Scripture is part of my praying. I try to read meditatively, letting a portion of what is written find root in me rather than trying to plow through a long section. This need not be an elaborate affair. The state of my schedule and my discipline being what it is, I don't always manage to open the Bible every morning. When I don't, I try at least to call up a memorized verse or passage. The goal is to allow God's truth to keep us from getting off track. One does not need a graduate degree to understand Scripture's plain (sometimes painfully plain) words.

Once we take in such truth, we naturally cry out to God. This spontaneous word spoken back to God becomes another step in listening prayer. So I often *pray* what I've read. I ask God to reveal himself, indeed, as my Shepherd. Or I ask him to make real a lesson in trusting him that I may have read about in a story like Abraham's. These responses include questions where fuller understanding is needed—"Lord, what are you saying to me today?"—as well as prayers of thanksgiving and praise and petitions for wisdom, understanding, and guidance through what I have read.

Then comes active listening to God.[8] We open ourselves to what God might want to say. We do not manipulate—God comes at his initiative, not our conjuring—but neither do we close our minds. Rather, we face the unnerving prospect that God may indeed want to tell us something. Or we listen with an uncontainable delight when God reminds us that he cares enough not to leave us alone in our decisions and questions.

❖⟨◆⟩❖

Through all this listening for God, I try to remember that guidance is sought only as part of a certain kind of life: one of loving, ongoing relationship with the Guide. It is not fortune-telling we are about. God's word is not something we call up only when we grow anxious. We do not ask for God's Spirit to guide us only when we *feel* uncertain. We do not make our goal so much extracting specific data on what to expect as much as gaining the Lord's mind. We seek an increase of the wisdom of the Lord.

And then we try to let what we read stay with us. In the same way that the early morning words of my wife will sometimes linger in my mind for much of the day, so the words of Scripture can carry me along. In the harried and hurried rush of many days, I don't always manage to listen attentively, or even to listen at all, but when I do, what I have heard can feed my soul with truth as I walk into the scenes of my life.

Even in the everydayness of ordinary life, sometimes Scripture will speak to us in a remarkably powerful way. My friend Kevin Miller once told me of the time his father died. By the time his mother called to tell him that his dad was in the hospital after a massive heart attack, the man had already been admitted to the coronary intensive care unit. "I went back to my bedroom," Kevin recalled. "I was really upset. But when I opened my Bible, I chanced to open the passage in Matthew 4 that spoke of Jesus's first disciples leaving their fathers to follow him. That phrase hit me. I realized that regardless of what happened with my dad, I had to follow Jesus. I heard a word that helped get me through a difficult time."

Listening takes discipline, sometimes a discipline I lack, but times spent in listening prayer keep me coming back to a God who is eager to communicate through every means imaginable. So I try to turn the ear of my soul toward this great God who is full of wisdom, a great God who is eager to speak.

Prayers

Lord, help me not to talk over you. Deliver me from chatter. Help me hear you when you speak in Scripture, help me see you in Jesus Christ, and enable me to follow all that your Holy Spirit leads me to. Amen.

Speak, Lord, for your servant hears.
Grant us ears to hear,
Eyes to see,
Wills to obey,
Hearts to love.

—CHRISTINA ROSSETTI, NINETEENTH CENTURY

MAKING SENSE OF
UNANSWERED PRAYERS

I have lived to thank God that all my prayers
have not been answered.

—JEAN INGELOW

Beware, in your prayer, above everything, of limiting God,
not only by unbelief, but by fancying that you know what
he can do.

—ANDREW MURRAY

Some years ago a friend gave me a biography of nineteenth-century British orphanage founder George Müller. What I read both heightened my expectancy for prayer and led me to some wondering and soul searching.

When I opened the book, I read how threadbare, scrawny orphans often begged on the streets of Müller's England. Sometimes the authorities packed them off to workhouse dungeons. Müller decided he had to help. He left his mark on history by pioneering a work that would eventually house and feed thousands of desperate children.

What especially struck me was the way Müller chose to finance his work: through prayer. He vowed that he would never talk about a need for food or buildings or money. He would "advertise" the necessities to

"no man"—only to God. In spite of some close scrapes, Müller's insistence on turning to God alone in prayer always seemed to "work"
somehow. On one such morning, he had gathered the children
around a breakfast table set with plates and cups, but no food. After
thanking God for the food "you are going to give us to eat," someone
knocked on the door. There stood a local baker saying, "I couldn't
sleep last night. Somehow I felt you didn't have bread for breakfast,
and the Lord wanted you to have some. So I got up at two o'clock and
baked some fresh bread." Almost immediately there came a second
knock. This time it was a milkman who announced that his milk cart
had broken down outside the orphanage. He wanted the children to
have his milk so he could empty his wagon and repair it.[1] In instance
after instance, when funds fell low, without fail an envelope of money
would come, often in the nick of time.

When I received Müller's biography, my wife and I were facing
some daunting circumstances of our own. We lived on a stringent
budget, and we never seemed to have money enough for each month's
bills. As we read about Müller, we remembered with a sense of hopelessness a bill we owed for income taxes. We thought the due date would
present the perfect occasion to put Müller's prayer principle to the test.
It could be an eleventh-hour breakthrough, some unforeseen gift or
windfall, but if we only asked, we reasoned, an answer would come.

I never will forget the mingled hope and trepidation with which
we greeted April 15. Nor will I forget what actually happened. More
precisely, what *didn't* happen.

No check made its way miraculously to our mailbox. No anonymous benefactor called. Our debt would plague us for months. As the
day wore on and our prospects for meeting our obligation became
bleaker, my wife and I wondered if we had misunderstood. Was God
not willing to do this sort of thing? Or were we just mistaken?

Practically anyone can tell of similar experiences. Nothing troubles
us more than the hurt or anger or confusion left in the wake of a

request that God, by all appearances, ignores. Not only will the door not open, it seems closed in our faces. And our requests seem so good, so sincere. Why the apparent cosmic indifference?

The problem of unanswered prayers is one of the most thorny facing those who pray. On one level, of course, we can all see why sometimes our petitions must go unmet. "If God answered the prayers of dogs," an Arabian proverb has it, "it would rain bones." When two Indiana high-school basketball teams face off in a state championship game, teammates on both sides pray with all that is in them—even making deals with God. We know that such prayers must always end in disappointment for someone. We have no trouble intellectually seeing that granting one side's requests means refusing the other side's.

But the intellect does not always answer for our feelings. In many experiences of asking, we find it hard not to feel snubbed. We could handle a mere no, but sometimes facing an unanswered prayer seems more like being slighted than merely refused. The most difficult part is not the denial as much as the fear that we have been ignored.

The nature of prayer itself doesn't help. Talk to a flesh-and-blood friend, and you can grasp a hand or peer into a pair of eyes. But prayer involves addressing a Presence we do not tangibly see or touch, a Person we rarely—or never—audibly hear. "I feel like Helen Keller in a barrel," someone once confessed to a friend. "Sometimes I feel like my prayers go nowhere." We cry out in agony or desperation, but the silence remains pointed and poignant.

I believe our uncertainty in these matters is both easily resolved and ultimately mysterious. On one level, explaining unanswered prayer means plumbing the depths of the problem of evil and pain. To be glib is to be cruel to those who still ache or wonder. But on another level, some simple points can make sense of most of our problems. I will touch on the latter, simpler answers before attacking the tougher, larger questions.

❧❧❧

Our wrestling with unanswered prayers has to do, first of all, with a fuzziness about what we can expect from God. "The real problem," says C. S. Lewis, "is…not why refusal is so frequent, but why the opposite result is so lavishly promised."[2] Why is the Bible so unrestrained in its promise of answers? We are told to pray in faith, believing. Ask, seek, knock, Jesus said, and you will be answered, you will find, the door will be opened. "You may ask me for anything in my name," Jesus promised his followers, "and I will do it" (John 14:14).

So what does seemingly unanswered prayer mean? What good is prayer if it is sometimes answered and sometimes not? Several reminders about the nature of prayer have helped in my own struggle with unanswered prayer and have encouraged me to keep praying even when I have been disappointed. These angles on prayer ultimately help me see how God uses—and does not use—our prayers.

Distinguish Between God's Long View and Our Timing

In our day of instant everything, we may be "quickaholics," as someone has aptly put it. Our culture conditions us to think that faster is always better, whether we are getting fitted for eyeglasses or grabbing a salad. Even in our spiritual hunger, we want microwave convenience. We prefer our answers—perhaps even answers from God—in sound bites.

This insistence on instancy affects even the church. In some religious quarters, it seems, the more abrupt a prayed-for change in someone is, the more certain you can be that you are witnessing the action of God. Suddenness functions as a seal of spiritual authenticity. But while conversion or healing or immersion in the reality of God certainly may happen by fiat, it is often the exception. We must usually trust the seemingly slow work of God. We must try not to give up easily.

I have planted seeds in a garden many times: pumpkin seeds, beans, zinnia seeds. Almost always they germinate and push up seedlings. When I have to wait and wait, though, I must resist the temptation to dig them up every couple of days to see how they are doing. To do so could stunt or kill the tender shoots. In spiritual matters I have also had to learn the value of deliberateness and calm steadiness. I must prepare to wait. I need to expect change in increments. Sometimes God's best answer is "Not now" or "Wait."

While Jill and I did not get the money we needed for our tax bill when we wanted it, we did manage to pay the debt off over the following several months. On paper, finding the extra money to pay the IRS looked impossible. But God was faithful. We just had to wait—and to learn some lessons about the long view.

For some things, an instant answer is unrealistic. When we pray that we will become more spiritually mature, we should not expect an immediate result. We will need to think in terms of months, not moments; decades, not days. Consider a woman who sees a chess set while shopping at a department store. She approaches a clerk and says, "This looks interesting. How do you play it?" Well, some answers are not reducible to a two-minute explanation. God does work miracles of immediate transformation in people, but development of character—for which we should most certainly pray—usually will not happen in a thunderclap. Pray for patience, and God's answer will likely be to place you in proximity to irritating people around whom you will have to fashion new ways of relating. Pray for more faith, and you may find yourself in the kinds of situations my wife and I faced with our finances.

So I may have to keep on praying—again and again. Sometimes I call to mind Englishman William Carey, a pioneer missionary in the early nineteenth century. Addressing his son, he once said that if after his death anyone found his life worth writing about, there was one criterion by which to judge an account's correctness: "If he give me credit for being a plodder he will describe me justly. Anything beyond this will be too much. I can plod. That is my only genius. I can persevere in any definite pursuit. To this I owe everything."[3]

Too often I quit when an answer does not immediately drop from the sky. But according to Jesus, persistence carries the day. One of the important things about prayer is to keep at it. Jesus painted some rather outlandish pictures (called parables) to drive the point home: Imagine God is like a friend to whom you go at midnight to borrow bread when relatives unexpectedly show up. Your friend hates the idea of getting out of bed and waking his children in the process. But you go on knocking anyway. He gives you what you want so he can go back to bed (see Luke 11:5-13). Or consider a callous judge, Jesus said. The judge cannot care less about your predicament as a widow, wronged in a society that shows little interest in the rights of widows. But just to get you out of his hair, he will hear your case and rule in your favor (see Luke 18:1-8). God may seem slow, but he's listening. *Don't give up,* Jesus tells us.

You may pray for years for triumph over some temptation. You may petition God for justice in some terrible situation. You ask for a loved one to be saved from addiction. Don't too quickly conclude that a lack of an immediately identifiable answer means nothing is happening. Keep praying, says Jesus, even when the years turn into decades and you still see no concrete evidence. Easier to say than to live, but some things take time.

Recognize God's Blessings for What They Are

We sometimes ask for possessions that would ruin us if we got them. Relationships that would drain us if we entered into them. Power that would corrupt us if we got it. The young boy who sees his mother carving the Thanksgiving turkey may plead for a chance to wield the knife himself. "No," the parent must say. And it may be years before the boy understands the reason. God treats us too well—and loves us too much—to give us some of the things we ask for.

So when we hear a "no" or a "wait," we remember that we don't always see clearly. I do not always recognize God's answers right off. Sometimes he responds—gloriously and obviously—with just what I want. Sometimes he gives me the desires of my heart. But I believe this happens most often when my will is in line with his. And when it is not, God in his graciousness withholds the desired object.

I like the story of a Chinese farmer who kept an old horse for tilling the fields. One day the horse escaped into the hills. When all the farmer's neighbors sympathized with him over his bad luck, he said, "Bad luck? Good luck? Who knows?"

A week later the horse returned with a herd of wild horses from the hills. This time the neighbors congratulated the farmer on his good luck. He replied, "Good luck? Bad luck? Who knows?"

When one of his sons was trying to tame one of the wild horses, he broke his leg. Everyone thought this very bad luck. Not the farmer, whose reaction was simply, "Bad luck? Good luck? Who knows?"

Some weeks later the army marched into the village and conscripted every able-bodied youth they could find. When they saw the farmer's son with his broken leg, they let him off. Now was that good luck or bad luck? Who knows?

So much that on the surface seems to be misfortune may be a benefit in disguise. And what seems like an unqualified good may cause our devastation. Our perspective is so limited. We are wise when we leave it to God to decide what is good "luck" and bad.

Value the Process of Praying More Than the Object of Request

God may be less concerned about answering the petition that forms on our lips than he is with shaping *us*. Prayer does sometimes change us. What drives us to prayer ultimately sets in motion a soul searching that leaves us changed. With time, what we "needed" may not seem so urgent, or even desirable. As our wills become more conformed to his, what we thought was so prized may pale or even seem wrong. I have prayed for jobs that I later blessed God for not allowing me to get. But God still brings good because the very process of praying helps me grow. In the case of my wife and me—praying with all our might for a miraculous influx of cash into our checking account—God had some deeper work to do. He taught us something about walking by faith, not by sight. He also let us learn some practical lessons about managing our finances.

⚜

Sometimes our impatience with unanswered prayer has to do with lost perspective in yet another sense: We forget the prayers that God has already answered. Clinging to our disappointment in a given situation may blind us to the miraculous we have already experienced. We forget that God *can* and *does* move in powerful ways in response to prayer.

This was true with my friend Jeanie Hunter. She told me this story:

> In 1983, surgery to have a tumor removed from my ear left a facial nerve severely damaged, causing paralysis and weakness on the left side of my face. My hearing was so affected that I had to wear a hearing aid. The nerve controlling taste was cut so that food tasted like wet cardboard. And my middle ear was injured, leaving a constant ringing. On top of all this, I was so dizzy I had to spend most of the day in bed or lying on a couch.
>
> On Wednesday, February 11, 1987, someone from my church called and asked if I was going to attend the Wednesday morning service. I said no—I tried not to be out of my office during the day, and besides, I wasn't feeling well. I had a sofa in my office and I intended to lie down. My friend, however, was not easily put off. She told me that a guest speaker with a healing ministry, Delores Winder, was going to speak. I finally agreed.
>
> As I drove to the church, I could sense a voice saying,

"This could be the last time you drive to the church sick." I knew the medical community had done all it could. Could it be possible that Jesus would heal me?

After Delores spoke, I went forward to ask her to pray with me. I explained my condition. She and a handful of prayer counselors prayed with me. My prayer was "Lord, please either heal me or let me die. I just cannot live with this illness any longer."

When I opened my eyes, I saw I was bathed in light. Then from the middle of the light, God sent a washing of love that penetrated every part of my being. As I stood in the light, it was as though I could see four-inch-tall letters that read, "YOU ARE HEALED."

Suddenly I found my hearing aid on my lap. For the first time I was able to hear without it. The noise in my head and the dizziness vanished. Feeling in my extremities and head returned. I could actually walk through a door without hitting the door frame. And taste! It came back in a little over a month, while I was licking envelopes in the office. That evening, as my daughter and I went up and down the aisles of the supermarket, I kept opening the packages as I threw them into the cart. I hadn't tasted food for four years, and I couldn't wait!

I believe it is important, in the midst of grappling with a seemingly unanswered prayer, to *remember* that God clearly does respond—dramatically—to prayer. In our disappointment we may too easily forget. We overlook what we have already received, the answers that have come, the "divine coincidences" that have accompanied so many requests.

This is why memory can be such an ally in the spiritual life. Recounting the blessings of the past gives us perspective on the present. When we forget what God has already done, life may seem aimless. Prayer may seem like a futile enterprise.

In *The Man Who Mistook His Wife for a Hat,* neurologist Oliver Sacks recounts the story of a man, Mr. Thompson, whose memory had been obliterated by Korsakov's syndrome. When Sacks visited him in the hospital, Mr. Thompson "would identify me—misidentify, pseudo-identify me—as a dozen different people in the course of five minutes. He would whirl, fluently, from one guess, one hypothesis, one belief, to the next.... He remembered nothing for more than a few seconds." Loss of memory completely disoriented Mr. Thompson. He built bridges across the "abyss of amnesia" that opened continually beneath him with fluent confabulations and fictions of all kinds, one moment speaking as a delicatessen-grocer and the next as an imaginary reverend. Sacks theorizes that "to be ourselves we must *have* ourselves—possess, if need be re-possess, our life-stories."[4] Without remembering, life—and prayer—seem random, topsy-turvy.

So sometimes, when God's answers seem slow, I try to recall his coming through in other difficult times. For instance, several years ago my family moved to a new community. Right up to the day of the move, and even beyond, we had settled little in terms of jobs or housing. Even though we had been unable to pull these vital elements together, my wife and I, supported by the wise counsel of friends, had a clear sense that we should move. During our preparations for the move, I would sometimes read through pages of my journals from previous years just to be reminded that God had been faithful in the past. That helped me believe that God could be trusted for the present. Recalling those earlier answers helped me not lose confidence that he was at work in my life.

That is why, I believe, the Bible speaks so often of memory. "I will remember the deeds of the LORD," wrote the psalmist. "Yes, I will remember your miracles of long ago" (77:11). Calling to mind God's prior faithfulness can be an antidote for spiritual depression. It keeps in perspective the seemingly unanswered prayer of the moment.

My friend Charlene Baumbich believes there is no such thing as unanswered prayer: "Perhaps God won't give me the answer I'm expecting, or answer *when* I'm expecting an answer, but I have come to learn that his sovereign hand is always wrapped around my life. I might box with God on occasion, just to relieve frustration over what seem like slow answers, but looking back over my life, I know he's always in my corner."

❖

But some would say these attempts to understand unanswered prayer do not truly satisfy. A nineteen-year-old, studying for the priesthood, gets cancer, and a chorus of prayers rises to God. But he dies, painfully, seemingly without sense, a promising life cut short. Or consider the Holocaust. Jewish theologian Martin Buber once asked, "Can one still speak to God after [the concentration camp of]...Auschwitz? Can one still, as an individual and as a people, enter at all into a dialogue relationship with Him? Dare we recommend to the survivors...the Jobs of the gas chambers, 'Call to Him, for He is kind, for His mercy endureth forever'?"[5]

The mystery of evil is great. There can be no glib answers to the achingly painful denials; the unanswered requests that leave us broken, devastated. When that happens, we have trouble even coming near God because of our disappointment.

Oxford don C. S. Lewis was one of the great theologians of the twentieth century. But Lewis lost his wife to cancer and wrestled profoundly with his grief. In his book *A Grief Observed,* he gave us glimpses of the struggle:

> Meanwhile, where is God?... Go to Him when your need is desperate, when all other help is vain, and what do you find? A door slammed in your face, and a sound of bolting and

double bolting on the inside. After that, silence.... There are
no lights in the windows.... It might be an empty house. Was
it ever inhabited?[6]

Is that the final word? When God refuses to intervene to save us
from suffering, is that the defining moment of his relationship with
us? Does he change from merciful Father to heartless rejecter?

Perhaps no one has asked such questions more poignantly than
the Old Testament figure Job. He lost it all, you could say: his family,
possessions, health. He has become a symbol of affliction. But even in
the midst of the heartache and unbelievable grief, Job considered it
unthinkable to turn away from God. God was still the center of Job's
existence. So he said, "Though [God] slay me, yet will I hope in him"
(Job 13:15). Job's experience with God and his memory of God's
faithfulness kept him from cursing God and giving up.

In many ways, Job received no explanation for his unanswered
prayers. God brought not explanations but himself. God, as the Bible
said, "answered Job out of the storm" (Job 38:1), not so much in specific answers to concrete requests, but by letting Job meet the
Answerer himself. Job found life filled with the gift of the Presence.
This appearance of God to Job brings an even greater climax to the
story than the chapter that closes the book, in which at the very end,
we see Job getting back all kinds of wealth in sheep and camels and
new children. God's appearance to Job climaxes the book because his
coming to Job was the ultimate response. Nothing could satisfy more
than knowing his life was held and surrounded by this God who
knew him and cared for him.

⊶⊰❖⊱⊷

One morning some years ago, I was summoned out of a board meeting for an emergency phone call. A hospital in Santa Monica had

called my wife with urgent news that my dad had been readmitted. He had had a severe heart attack just three weeks earlier, had partially recovered, and had been sent home. Indeed, I was scheduled to fly out the next day for a visit. But early that morning he had had another attack, and this time it looked as if he might not survive longer than a few hours.

I hopped on a plane in Chicago and headed for L.A. I so hoped Dad would survive at least until I got there. I wanted to tell him one last time that I loved him. I felt there was still some resolving to be done, especially in light of the break we experienced in our relationship years earlier. We had talked on the phone since his heart attack, but I wanted to *see* him. And there had been no chance for him to tell me about the arrangements he had made for Mom, who was hopeless with anything related to finances. It seemed like such a simple thing. So logical. So easy for God. "Please, Lord," I wrote in my journal not long before my plane landed, "keep Dad alive until I come."

I was greeted at the airport terminal by my mom and a friend of the family. It took but an instant to read their faces and hear what I had dreaded: Dad had died even as I was winging my way home. My prayer was not answered.

But that is not what I remember most about that time. While I certainly shed tears, while I regretted that I had missed seeing my dad one last time, God answered me with his presence. God drew close. He held me during a dark time.

The answer that matters more than any other is knowing we are not alone. In God we find assurance. We discover that whatever the specific outcome, we can know still the promise of One who said, "Lo, I am with you always." We may never "solve" the mystery of evil. We may not receive the reprieve or healing or break we hoped for, but in prayer we meet a Presence who can carry us through the pain of what seems to be a meager answer. With God by our side, we find the ultimate Answer.

PRAYERS

Lord, I want not to storm your door and demand an answer.
But I am anxious. I am waiting. If you will not bring what
I'm asking for, please bring You. Amen.

───◈───

Then Job replied to the LORD:
"I know that you can do all things;
*   no plan of yours can be thwarted.*
You asked, 'Who is this that obscures my counsel without
*   knowledge?'*
Surely I spoke of things I did not understand,
*   things too wonderful for me to know....*
My ears had heard of you
*   but now my eyes have seen you."*

—JOB 42:1-3,5

When Praying
Seems Impossible

O God…my soul thirsts for you, my body longs for you,
in a dry and weary land where there is no water.

—Psalm 63:1

The profit and increase in spiritual life comes not only
when you have devotion, but rather, when you can humbly
and patiently bear the withdrawal and absence of devotion,
yet not cease your prayers or leave undone your other customary good works.

—Thomas à Kempis,
The Imitation of Christ

On a hot summer day some years ago, I went to the kitchen for
a drink of water. But the faucet would only sputter. After a few
spurts, there was nothing. A drought had bled dry the underground
spring that fed the pipes in our rural Virginia home. Now I was *really*
thirsty. Sweaty and dry-mouthed, I began craving what I could not
have.

The discomfort and desperation that accompanied my physical
thirst finds a parallel in the spiritual life. Thirst is a powerful image for
our desire for God, our need for replenishment within the dry depths

of our spirits. Sometimes our life with God has the loamy moistness of a forest floor on a rainy day. We feel like a well-watered garden. But our prayer life can also feel like a desert. We try to pray but find we have nothing to say. Our souls resemble arid plains. Or we may be ready to talk, but it seems as if God has gone into hiding or, worse yet, that he has deserted us. At other times we sense God, but distractions war against our focus. Trying to pray becomes such a battle that we give it up.

More than we like to admit, prayer sometimes seems difficult and unrewarding. But that is precisely when we need to hang in there, to push past the obstacles.

When You Can't Concentrate

Often we sit down to pray and find our minds wandering. In my teaching and preaching about prayer over the years and in my conversations about prayer with many people, I find that this struggle with distraction is nearly universal. Perhaps the distraction appears as something simple, such as the teenage kid next door practicing electric guitar with window-rattling decibels or the couple in the apartment upstairs having another yelling binge.

One day my morning run took me off the road into wilder, undeveloped land. I wound along a dirt path to a stand of trees. There the canopy of branches overhead and carpet of undergrowth below became a kind of sanctuary. I grew still and quiet. Unfortunately, mosquitoes were also meditating there. They soon discovered my perspiration-soaked legs. Their buzzing and biting quickly brought my spiritual reverie to a halt. "I throw myself down in my Chamber," wrote poet John Donne in 1621, "and I...invite God and his angels thither, and when they are there, I neglect God and his angels for the noise of a fly, for the rattling of a coach, for the whining of a door."[1]

At other times we are no sooner settled to pray in a quiet, still place than we think of something that "has" to get done. Or we can't stop wondering how our mortgage will get paid. Wandering thoughts usually have more to do with what is going on deep within us than with interruptions from the outside. They have to do with our own cluttered inner closets.

Like few other things, prayer reveals to us how unfocused our lives are. We are busied and worried by many things. Overcoming the problem of scattered praying, then, requires more than devotional discipline. We need to examine our *lives*. What is the fundamental purpose of our living and striving? It is not that what we do day in and day out is unimportant or useless. Nor does God expect us to withdraw from the civilized world. It is more a matter of clarifying the focus of our urgency, the center of our attention. When Jesus told his listeners to seek first the kingdom of God (see Matthew 6:33), he was telling them (and us) that instead of worrying about the many things, we should concentrate on the one necessary thing. Jesus reminds us that our lives can be single-minded, not scattered. Instead of playing to the crowd, we live for the Audience of One. I cannot even hint that I have "arrived" when it comes to living out this goal. But I can remind myself that when I settle that I am living for God, at least some of the distractions will fall away. We carry on our daily work with our purpose more sure, and we go back to our praying with our reasons more defined.

Another reason distractions throw us off has to do with our worry about how prayer "feels." We measure its "effectiveness" by the minutes of concentrated focus. But our subjective impressions of our prayer times may not be correct. Indeed, a seemingly futile prayer time may be more significant than we know. "For this reason," argues Tad Dunne,

> it is important to pay some attention to "distractions" in prayer. They may be the real prayer, while the words we were mumbling are really distraction. A "distraction" will be genuine prayer insofar as it arises out of a sufficiently deep sense of wonder about something in our experience. The "prayer"

may in reality be the distraction insofar as we use it to avoid facing life as it comes.[2]

So we pray through our seeming distractions, trusting that below and behind our scattered processes a great unseen work is still being done. We pray by faith, not by sight. We believe that prayer matters even when we do not feel every moment spent in prayer comes with unruffled clarity. God is more concerned about a heart that is turned toward him than about a mind that is neatly ordered and stoically calm.

One morning years ago I sat down, as I do so many mornings, to pray. Wanting to let my wife sleep in, I soon had a very awake five-year-old yelling for maple "oartmeal." Once I had Bekah settled with bowl and spoon, I slipped off to another room, my Bible and journal and prayer list in hand. I managed a few moments of prayer before she found me. I enjoyed having her snuggle against me while she watched television, but a time of uninterrupted peace it was not. Even when I eventually got alone again, I had trouble getting my mind off the previous day's projects at work. I had trouble concentrating.

And yet I prayed. While I would not memorialize it as a watershed of charged spiritual passion, real prayer took place. God was pleased. My effort was not in vain.

It is said that once when Martin Luther's dog happened to be near the table, the dog noticed with open mouth what Luther was eating. Luther commented, "Oh, if I could only pray the way this dog watches the meat! All his thoughts are concentrated on the piece of meat. Otherwise he has no thought, wish, or hope." We can get better at concentrating. Progress is possible. Although we are always beginners in prayer, we can still form new habits. We can establish new grooves. Our minds and bodies are wonderfully designed to respond to exercise and discipline. Just as our biceps and calf muscles grow stronger with exertion, so can our spiritual faculties. We can take advantage of some practical ways to minimize the distraction of distractions in our prayer life. Getting up early in the morning (or staying up late at night) helps me here. At times in my life, I could beat the rest of the household (at least the kids) by setting my alarm early. Even fifteen minutes in the living room to gather my thoughts and pray can make a difference in any day. Other times I have been able to draw away from the distraction of e-mail or the latest *Newsweek* on the coffee table by going for a run in the neighborhood, trying while I put one foot in front of the other to pray.

I also try to keep my praying simple. Meditatively, slowly reciting a memorized prayer such as the Lord's Prayer may help. I also try to begin by simply stating that I want to talk to God and be in loving relationship to him. Remembering that prayer is ultimately about *God* and not forms or formulas can give our prayer a spaciousness that allows us to rise above the frantic pace of our sometimes driven minds.

And I find value in varying the routine. There is no reason to lock in a prescribed pattern if a change of pace occasionally helps you not get bored or distracted. Someone once told me of how, for a time, he got tired of "praying in the usual way every night." So for a year or so, he and his wife would sing a hymn every night. "We kept a hymnbook by our bed. We would pick a hymn, sometimes one that seemed to especially fit what we were experiencing, and sing it as a prayer." We need not worry about there being only one "right" way to pray.

When Praying Seems Uneven

Because prayer is largely about a relationship and has so much to do with intangibles such as desire and faith, we sometimes like to think that no work or discipline will be necessary. We prefer spontaneity. And there are those times when something wonderful just "happens." The words come to us. The longing for God rises without coaxing. Praying seems effortless.

But no relationship can be built solely on impromptu utterances. We must also at times add diligence. Sometimes we must work at it. "The only way to pray is to pray," writes spiritual teacher Dom John Chapman, "and the way to pray well is to pray much. If one has no time for this, then one must at least pray regularly. But the less one prays, the worse it goes. And if circumstances do not permit even regularity, then one must put up with the fact that when one does try to pray, one can't pray—and our prayer will probably consist of telling this to God."[3] We cannot get by without some constancy and consistency.

So sometimes I find that I raise myself out of bed in the morning to pray whether I *feel* like it or not. I try to read the Bible whether it is my first choice of reading material or not.

I tell myself that periodically we all need to stand back from the filigree of our daily schedules and look at the broad strokes and overall composition of our personal world. I believe that every life will benefit from regular Bible reading. I believe most people should schedule regular time for prayer. Disciplines like keeping a prayer journal and reading the insights of spiritual writers may also help. The "big picture" settled, we carry out the particulars whether or not feelings always follow.

And then following disciplines helps untie us from our attachment to the many things in our lives. Fasting, the conscious decision to do without food for a morning or day (in rare cases, longer), can help us focus on God. It can free us from our temptation to give food and its pleasure too much power over us. Or, taking seriously the admonition of the Bible not to "give up meeting together" (Hebrews 10:25), we resolve to attend church every week and observe the day of worship as a fast from work. Perhaps we give up some cherished food during a liturgical season such as Lent, believing that doing so can help sharpen our spiritual perception and free us to focus more effectively on spiritual matters.

There is another side to all this, of course. Thinking about discipline, resolving to pray regularly even when our hearts seem spiritually dry, sometimes leaves us uneasy. For one thing, we know our track record is mixed, as the countless exercise bikes gathering dust in garages across the country attest. Our plans to pray more regularly go the way of New Year's resolutions or the latest fad diet. We start and stop often.

We also know, instinctively or from firsthand observation, how disciplines can become legalisms. Rather than providing simple form and structure, our exercises stifle us. They become a burden. We become weighed down, even fearful of not following through. We can become wedded to our programs, convinced that true spirituality will come with just one more technique, one more sacrifice. We forget that practices should always be seen as means, not ends. The aim is not to rack up points for heroic effort, but to grow closer to God.

I don't consider myself exceptionally disciplined. I recognize the value of exercise and I run some mornings, but I never log my running times and miles. I run four times one week and one time the next. I know I should read the classics of literature, but I have started (but not finished) Dostoyevsky's *The Brothers Karamazov* more times than I like to admit. And I find it much the same when it comes to prayer.

So it's not surprising that I have failed at some of my more ambitious attempts to be disciplined in prayer. Reading about one man's commitment to pray an hour every day, for example, once inspired me to do the same—for about two weeks. I appreciate those who organize their devotions with Day-Timers and checklists. I've tried with my share of alarm-blasting mornings to do the same. And while I keep a spiritual journal to record what I think God is saying to me, the frequency is erratic. I have come to believe that some of us will never be zealously organized and wonderfully disciplined in our praying because we don't approach any aspect of our lives that way. Our temperaments are different.

A friend of mine confessed, "I simply have not been able to become more disciplined about following some kind of regimented schedule. But," she continued, "I don't think I'm falling terribly short on this. I talk to God in the midst of anything and everything, whether for a passing moment in the midst of doing the laundry, while giving a speech, or actually kneeling in prayer." I don't think my friend has plumbed the depths of spiritual practice, but she senses the need for a kind of unconstricted approach that gives her freedom and delight. And she is on the way to a fuller life.

One man came up to author Steve Brown and said he needed help with developing a regular prayer life. "I really want to have that time," he said, "but I've tried to start and have quit even more times than I've tried to quit smoking. Can you help me?"

"I told him," recalls Steve, "that…in his enthusiasm for having a time of prayer, he was overcommitting himself. I suggested that he take no more than five or ten minutes each morning to read a passage of Scripture, to spend some time telling God how wonderful he is and thanking him for all he has done, to confess all the sins he could remember, to pray the Lord's Prayer, and to pray about the things that bothered him. 'Then quit,' I said. 'Don't increase the time you spend until it is absolutely necessary that you increase it. Don't go beyond the ten minutes until you simply can't stay within the ten minutes.' That simple advice absolutely changed his walk with God. Now he can accurately be described as a man of prayer."[4]

Praying regularly may not be easy, but it gets easier. We establish some habits that become familiar. We may even gain a certain pleasure from the predictability. One week not long ago, I began each morning with a half-hour run. I had gotten submerged in so much busyness in the preceding weeks that I had had little exercise. I was out of shape. That first day when I ran, my body dragged. I wanted to be somewhere else, doing anything but picking up my heavy feet, pushing my tired body, taxing my reluctant lungs.

But I noticed something as the week progressed. The running became more natural, less of an effort. I started to look forward to each run.

Around the same time, a friend shared an insight from a conference he attended on the spiritual life. Becoming more disciplined in your prayer life will feel at first like you're swimming upstream, he had heard a teacher say. It will be hard work. But if you keep at it, someday the current will suddenly reverse directions—and it will carry you along, if you let it.

When Prayer Seems Bone Dry

No matter how rich and full our praying may seem when we begin, most of us move into feelingless, arid stretches. "In the beginning," wrote a friend of his times in God's presence, "I was surprised to be deeply 'touched' emotionally [during] each prayer time. I took that as a sign that something was happening in me. I was spurred on by the results." But then something changed. "Now it seems as if there are no feelings other than intermittent impatience with being in a place that feels barren."

Those who take prayer seriously commonly go through a period, sometimes a long period, when they experience the apparent absence of God. The warm flush of feelings vanishes.

This may be tied, first of all, to barrenness in our emotional lives. When nerves fray and calm unravels, we may find it noticeably harder to pray. The loss of a child, the pain of a divorce, a diagnosis of serious illness—such things can so shatter our composure that we find all our routines upset.

More commonly, I believe that bouts of dryness in prayer have to do with spiritual dynamics. The ways we have previously thought about God suddenly seem shallow. We undergo a purifying of our conceptions of God. But as we are letting go of the old ways of seeing him, after perhaps fashioning him in our own image, God seems absent or even nonexistent. We feel as if we are "beating on Heaven's door with bruised knuckles in the dark," to use pastor and writer George Buttrick's phrase.[5] Whether we call it a spiritual dry spell or a "dark night of the soul," the results can be startling and discouraging. A person may even doubt his or her faith.

Ironically, such times may actually be a sign of deepening faith, in which the soul is seeking for a more genuine knowledge of God and broaching untested ideas about God. We let go of the superficial faith that got us by for a while. And while something deeper and more profound is growing in its place, the *sensation* is barrenness. God is withering our confidence in our old ways of relating. Or perhaps God has withdrawn the sense of his presence so we recognize its sweetness when it returns. The letting go of the familiar creates pain.

How do we make our way through such times? One way is simply not to give up. We carry on. I was impressed by the way my friend Cathy coped: "Even in the dry, desert experience of this past summer, I would take the time that was 'designated' as prayer time and at least 'show up.' Maybe all I did was sit, but I found that the sitting itself was prayer, that the important part was that I set aside the time to be in total attentiveness to God."

Sometimes I try to make the dryness a prayer in itself by acknowledging it before God. I offer it to him. I try to remember that, as contemplative writer Thomas Merton noted, "There is no such thing as a prayer in which 'nothing is done' or 'nothing happens,' although there may well be a prayer in which nothing is perceived or felt or thought."[6]

A woman I know told me that during a particularly stressful time in her marriage, "I was hurting so bad, things in my life were so crazy, I couldn't pray. I didn't know what to ask for. I felt so alone. So some nights I just sang the child's song 'Jesus Loves Me.' It was such a simple song, but I could sing that until I fell asleep. I knew God would honor that. The least little bit, he'll honor that."[7]

So we slog through. And as we do, we recall that we are not alone, even if we feel so. We pray in the faith that God not only hears our dry prayers but he helps us through them:

> Blessed is the man who trusts in the LORD,
>   whose confidence is in him.
> He will be like a tree planted by the water
>   that sends out its roots by the stream.

It does not fear when heat comes;
    its leaves are always green.
It has no worries in a year of drought
    and never fails to bear fruit. (Jeremiah 17:7-8)

When We Feel Harassed

I should end this chapter with a caution: We occasionally encounter in prayer (and in life) something even more unsettling than dryness. We face times for which mere persistence will not be sufficient. During such times we gain glimpses that we are engaged in a battle for which nothing less than supernatural resources will do.

Someone I'll call Bill works at a printing plant. During his freshman year of college, Bill experienced wonderful growth in his faith. He loved to pray, so much so that he sometimes had trouble waiting for class to be done so that he could get back to his room to pray.

But one day, he recounts, "I rested my head on my desk to close my eyes and pray. Immediately it was as though I was looking down a dark tunnel. I could 'see' threatening faces and heard, in my imagination, eerie, screaming voices. It was like a horror movie."

The hideous images continued for several hours, every time he closed his eyes to pray. "It was so obvious it was a spiritual attack," he says. "I felt that demons were trying to keep me from praying. Finally, as I claimed that Christ had authority, the images stopped. I felt peace. I could go to bed and actually sleep."

Prayer cannot always be gentle and calm. Sometimes it is a battle. Sometimes Sunday-school prayers of the meek-and-mild-Jesus variety are not enough. We should not hesitate to pray militantly, boldly, whenever we see ourselves or someone else harassed by the demonic. We live in what C. S. Lewis called "enemy-occupied territory": "Christianity is the story of how the rightful king has landed, you might say in disguise, and is calling us all to take part in a great campaign of sabotage."[8]

This explains why biblical writers sometimes used images of war when describing our spiritual work. "Put on the full armor of God so that you can take your stand against the devil's schemes," we read in Ephesians 6:11.

Evil not only exists, it works with persuasive and intensely personal power. For centuries spiritual writers have seen demons as more than metaphor, the devil as more than symbol. All that inhabits the spiritual realm is not pure and good. In prayer we face off against spiritual forces malign in intention. David Bolt writes,

> Anyone who has ever tried to formulate a private prayer in silence, and in his own heart, will know what I mean by diabolical interference. The forces of evil are in opposition to the will of God. And the nearer a [person] approaches God's will, the more apparent and stronger and more formidable this opposition is seen to be. It is only when we are going in more or less the same direction as the devil that we are unconscious of any opposition at all.[9]

Evil indeed taunts us with a seductive voice and oily reasoning. It arises within us, yet we also know it as a force outside of us. When Jesus began his ministry, he was led into a wilderness to be tempted by the devil (see Matthew 4:1-11). He was harassed by a malevolence that wielded ingenious subtlety and persistent logic. When Jesus sent his followers to the surrounding towns preaching and healing, he warned them they would be "lambs among wolves" (Luke 10:3). Peter, one of Jesus's first followers, later cautioned a first-century gathering of believers that "Your enemy the devil prowls around like a roaring lion looking for someone to devour" (1 Peter 5:8). The supernatural realm warrants care and discernment, lest we sweep out the clutter in our inner lives only to have it reoccupied by that which is even worse. Even Satan can masquerade as an "angel of light," the Bible tells us (2 Corinthians 11:14).

We should not be alarmed when prayer requires that we don the armor of faith or call out to God in Jesus's name for the power of the Holy Spirit. To talk of the devil not only explains our experience; it also exposes our enemy. So we need not delay in calling on God's limitless power when we "pray against" temptation in all its many varieties: addiction, lust, greed, deception—all of which would enslave and destroy what God created to be free and holy. We pray, "Lord, in Jesus's powerful name, we invite you to act in this situation." And we turn to Scripture: "For the word of God is living and active. Sharper than any double-edged sword, it penetrates even to dividing soul and spirit, joints and marrow; it judges the thoughts and attitudes of the heart" (Hebrews 4:12). We find promises in God's Word of his vanquishing power over evil and the demonic, and we live and pray in the confidence these promises bring.

And, I believe, if throughout our praying our goal remains to look to God and think of him, we need not worry. The Bible tells us that Jesus disarmed the demonic powers, making a public spectacle of them through the cross (see Colossians 2:15). God can be trusted to be our strength. God can drive out that which would plague our thoughts or poison our praying. After telling the early church to "test the spirits to see whether they are from God," the writer of the New Testament letter 1 John reminded his hearers, "You…are from God and have overcome them, because the one who is in you is greater than the one who is in the world" (4:1,4). The cross and resurrection of Jesus show that God is victorious over the forces of evil and death. And that is a victory in which we can share.

PRAYERS

Lord, I thank you for your great power made vivid in Jesus. May his love keep me on the straight path and his strength make me safe from all harm. Amen.

Why, O Lord, is it so hard for me to keep my heart directed toward you? Why do the many little things I want to do, and the many people I know, keep crowding my mind, even during the hours that I am totally free to be with you and you alone?...Do I keep wondering, in the center of my being, whether you will give me all I need if I just keep my eyes on you?

Please accept my distractions, my fatigue, my irritations, and my faithless wanderings. You know me more deeply and fully than I know myself. You love me with a greater love than I can love myself. You even offer me more than I desire. Look at me, see me in all my misery and inner confusion, and let me sense your presence in the midst of my turmoil.

—Henri J. M. Nouwen, *A Cry for Mercy*

DISCOVERING MODEL PRAYERS

The child learns to speak because his father speaks to
him.... So we learn to speak to God because God has
spoken to us and speaks to us. By means of the speech of
his Father in heaven his children learn to speak to him.
Repeating God's words after him, we begin to pray to him.

—DIETRICH BONHOEFFER, *Psalms*

Some years ago my son took piano lessons. Micah has always
had musical aptitude. He's good. But sometimes he complained
about the scales and arpeggios and cadences. They seemed like drudg-
ery. And reading a new piece of music was usually not as fun as playing around with blues runs. So I told him to "go ahead and improvise,"
but not all the time. Making up riffs has its limits. His fingers needed
the dexterity that comes from repetition. Certain techniques could
come only with long hours of lessons and practice. When he tired of
his own experimenting, I said, the quarter rests and eighth notes his
teacher drilled into him could open up a new world of music.

That we are made to pray does not mean we never need to "practice." Sometimes we need to do more than improvise. Our prayers
need sound instruction. When I run low on words, I need the kind
of grounding in good habits that Micah's piano lessons gave him. I
need teachers. I need to spend time with the prayers of others until I

gain a sense of them. Then my own prayers will have greater fluency and depth.

Jesus's disciples came to their Teacher and said, "Teach us to pray." They might as well have been speaking for us—for me. I need help with my fumbling words and sometimes awkward silences. I don't want to make prayer an exercise in rote woodenness, but I also know I need a model or pattern when words don't exactly roll off my tongue. I don't want always to have to figure out my prayers from scratch. Fortunately, I can find help from a host of resources and practices.

In the long history of faithful spiritual teachers, for example, not only do we find teaching *about* prayer; we see real people *praying*. So we take notes. We observe the words they used and the way they used them. We let our words fall into rhythm with theirs. We mimic the painter's strokes. Imitation is not only a form of flattery; it is a way to learn.

A part of us may hesitate, however. Sometimes we are not so sure about written or recited prayers. We may find them off-putting, akin, as Richard Foster writes, "to meeting an old friend on the street and quickly thumbing through a textbook to find an appropriate greeting."[1] But a book of prayers, the left-behind prayer jottings of history's spiritual pioneers, often helps me. I don't always want to come up with the words. Sometimes I *can't*. I need to be stretched sometimes by the good insights of other pray-ers.

⁘❖⁘

Scripture offers some of the most ancient prayers possible. When we pray Scripture, we can start with the prayers that others have proved and used before us, each word, as Eugene Peterson writes, "carrying the experience of generations."[2] Even better, by praying Scripture, God's revealed Word, we form the words of our prayers after God's very words.

Indeed, one of the most transforming insights for my praying came with the discovery that Scripture could not only be read but also *prayed.* I began to approach the Bible as a prayer book. I prayed using the actual words of Scripture. I watched Jesus model an astounding familiarity with God, calling God *Abba* (Aramaic for "Daddy" or "Father"). Emboldened by Jesus's example, I did too. Or I read Paul's words to the Ephesians in the New Testament, about his prayer that God would give his listeners "the Spirit of wisdom and revelation, so that [they] may know him better" (1:17). I saw him asking that the "eyes of [their] heart[s] may be enlightened in order that [they] may know the hope to which he has called [them], the riches of his glorious inheritance" (verse 18). I began to take such passages and fill in the names of friends, or even use them in prayers for myself. I had the feeling of repeating God's words after him, just as a child learns to speak through imitation. I had the feeling that I was praying not only at God's invitation but with his coaching. This gave me new confidence.

I also learned about "praying the promises." When God, speaking through the biblical writers and characters, promised some good thing or declared some immutable blessing, I took him at his word. I came to God saying, "This is what you promised." My prayers started with what I already knew God wanted to do.

Then I discovered the Bible's collection of psalms. I started rummaging around in all 150 poems and promises and worship choruses. Many of the psalms are, in fact, explicit prayers. The whole collection, called the Psalter, carries with it the inflections and rhythms of praise, worship, anguish, anger, hope, confession, and shame. It is, in other words, patently true to life, true to *my* life. In the thick of day-to-day living, to be able to call to mind a snatch of a psalm— "[Your] steadfast love endures forever" (136:1, NRSV) or "Lord, you have been our dwelling place throughout all generations" (90:1)—has made all the difference in how I've moved through an anxious time. Many mornings, as I have sat down, aware of the time and my need to get going, I have opened to a psalm and found myself slowing down, praying something I never would have thought of. I understand why Martin Luther said centuries ago of other ways of praying, "Ah, there is not the juice, the strength, the passion, the fire which I find in the Psalter."

Memorizing Scripture also helps me pray. It allows God's Word to bring form and beauty to my own sometimes artless praying. Waiting in a store checkout line or trying to go to sleep at night can become opportunities to think about the promises of God. The passages we select need not be lengthy; indeed, it is best if they are not. Right now I am memorizing John 14:21, in which Jesus says, "Whoever has my commands and obeys them, he is the one who loves me. He who loves me will be loved by my Father, and I too will love him and show myself to him." As I memorize and recite Scripture, I try to pray my way into the meaning and let the words suggest prayers, such as "Help me, Lord, obey you" or "Show yourself to me, Jesus."

Perhaps no prayer of Scripture better guides our sometimes fumbling or stuttered words than the Lord's Prayer, or, as it is known in some traditions, the Our Father. Found in Matthew 6 and Luke 11, this is the prayer Jesus gave his followers when they asked him to teach them to pray. It must be the most often quoted prayer in the Bible—and with good reason. Here Jesus touches on the great themes of praying: praise, confession, and petition. When we begin to plumb its depths, we will discover that it is far more than a hastily recited, rote prayer done as pure ritual.

The petitions of the Lord's Prayer, I find, can give my longings focus, helping me think through the issues and urgencies of the day. When someone asked a nineteenth-century spiritual teacher about cultivating a deeper prayer life, she replied, "Say the Lord's Prayer, but take an hour to say it." Here is how, as recorded in one of my recent journal entries, I allowed this model prayer to guide me through a rich morning prayer time:

Our Father in heaven. It's good to know you are in "heaven," Lord, that whatever else that means, you are above the push and pull of my little world. That you are aware of all that happens in the world around me.

Hallowed be your name. Lord, you are to be revered. Even your name is sacred. Help me hallow it—treating it as holy and sacred.

Your kingdom come. All the goodness and mercy and strength that make up your rule, Lord, help that come into being on earth.

Your will be done. May your plans not be hindered by others. May your purposes find no obstacle in me. I want to be willing.

On earth as it is in heaven. I pray that my actions will more closely resemble your heavenly designs.

Give us this day our daily bread. Lord, you know my family's need for food, for shelter, for transportation. Help me not to forget how my job helps provide for our daily needs. And help me always depend first on you and your generosity.

Forgive us our trespasses, as we forgive those who trespass against us. Lord, I need your forgiveness. I admit that I get caught up in stresses and pressures, that I do not always keep my focus on you. And I have been cranky with my family. Forgive me. And help me to forgive Anna, who hurt me needlessly.

Lead us not into temptation. Help me make choices today for the good.

But deliver us from evil. I count on your help! I need your Holy Spirit's power to save me from myself.

For thine is the kingdom, and the power, and the glory, forever.
Lord, it means so much to serve such a gracious God who
holds the world in his hands!

I find such a guide helpful when I am lying in bed, unable to
sleep at night, or when I get up in the morning. Or when I find my
mind wandering. Or when my self-made prayers seem to grind into
a rut. "To this day," sixteenth-century spiritual leader Martin Luther
once said, "I am still nursing myself on the Lord's Prayer like a child
and am still eating and drinking of it like an old man without getting
bored with it." Our praying of the Lord's Prayer need not be a slavish
occupation. And we need not pray the whole prayer each time. It
sometimes happens that I get so caught up in one of the petitions that
I forgo the others. Many are the times I have gotten no further than
"Our Father in heaven."

⊹❖⊹

The ways to give shape to our longing to converse with God are
many. Prayer books, such as *The Book of Common Prayer* of the Episcopal Church, provide a wealth of raw material for praying.

An acquaintance was talking the other day about times he
struggles a bit to pray. He recently spent several days in the hospital,
gravely ill yet buoyed up by the presence of God. And he found his
prayers enriched by *The Book of Common Prayer*. He was saying how
much it helped him when he wasn't feeling especially eloquent. "Praying those prayers," he said, "gives me the words for what I want to say
but can't always find the words for."

Many such books of prayers include prayers for morning and
evening, for the church seasons, even for times of birth or death.
Some prayer books are focused on particular themes, such as mother-
hood or college graduation. Others are collections of hundreds of

prayers throughout the centuries and across many cultures. Daily devotional guides or prayer calendars can help as well.

I like to experiment with these myriad ways of praying. For a period of some weeks, I may find the Lord's Prayer the most helpful basis for praying, using it with emphasis on praise and intercessory prayer for others. Other weeks I follow a monthly cycle of psalms (such as that found in *The Book of Common Prayer*). Or for a time I will read through a passage of Scripture a day, trying not only to assimilate its meaning but to understand the passage's relevance for the day's prayers. Sometimes I open the Bible and read only until something strikes me; then I pause and try to make the insight something I live with (and live out) during the day.

⁕⚜⁕

There is yet another way we benefit from the prayers of others: actually praying *with* people. The notion that prayer is only what we do when we are alone, the solo soul before God, may limit our prayers as much as an insistence on always "making them up." We live in an individualistic age in which the assumption is that a solitary walk in the woods is better for the soul than meeting with others.

But if left to myself, in spite of all my praying, my prayers become imbalanced or stuck. I need a way to avoid letting the eccentricities of my personal faith take me too far offtrack or get me caught in a rut. I also tend to get bogged down in my emotions. And feelings, as Eugene Peterson notes, can be the "scourge of prayer. To pray by feelings is to be at the mercy of glands and weather and indigestion. And there is no mercy in any of them."[3] My moods are too fickle to be reliable guides for the entirety of my spiritual life. And besides, there is a world of reality that I am too small to see by myself. I need the expanding of vision that praying with others brings. Prayer needs the soil of community to put down roots and flourish.

So when I come to worship in a blue funk, it does me good to join in a congregation's choruses of alleluias. Or I may be feeling cocky, convinced that all is well with the world and me. I need the reminder of prayers of confession that I still stumble and desperately need God's forgiveness. Perhaps I am complacent, living as I do in a comfortable house and a pleasant neighborhood. I need to be called to intercession for the world's hungry and poor.

And when I feel spiritually dry, when I don't feel particularly fluent or spiritual, I can be carried along by the momentum of a worship service. My words can find new footing. There is great comfort sometimes in "being led" in prayer. Someone stands in front of us and not only invites us to pray; he or she helps us actually find the words, words that we might never find within our narrow heart space. Suddenly it is not up to us. Our egos are no longer front and center. The corporate focus of worship—God—assumes center stage. Liturgy, the technical word for the way churches order their worship, is, as priest and author Simon Tugwell writes, "essentially something given, and in this it expresses a fundamental feature of all prayer. Its sublime lack of concern for our personal moods is a forcible reminder that when we come to God, it is not to force our moods or our interests on to him, but to receive his interests and to let him, in a sense, share his moods with us."[4]

❖

We find help in the prayers of others in yet another way. Perhaps it is no accident that many of the corporate prayers of synagogue and church throughout the centuries have incorporated music. Song brings our prayers into rhythm and harmony with others. Through the music and singing of corporate worship, we join our voices to theirs, and our own words find new patterns that we could never have devised by ourselves. Praying with others, sometimes *singing* those prayers in hymns and other worship songs, reminds us how much we need the voices and presence of one another to make a go of prayer. I remember once seeing a slogan on the office door of a choir director that read, "He who sings prays twice." The idea was that singing itself can be an act of prayer, in addition to whatever words of prayer appear in the song or hymn. Perhaps that slogan holds even truer when we sing our prayers with others. What we say not only gets shaped and formed by what we hear around us, but our sung prayers become a mighty voice of united longing and asking.

I suppose that Micah could have learned a certain amount of piano on his own, just as I might be able to pull together some kind of makeshift spiritual life as a hermit. But I knew Micah would never go far by himself, with his unguided improvising. He needed the weekly prodding and encouragement of his teacher. He needed her to pick out the songs and listen to Micah play them until he got them right. And when he hit an impasse, his instructor could take him to the next level. She kept his music from devolving into mere meandering.

It is remotely possible, I suppose, to make prayer a purely private enterprise. Possible, perhaps, but certainly not satisfying. Our lone voice does not a congregation or chorus make. I'll remember that the next time I think I can get by for long without others, and their prayers.

PRAYERS

Lord, help my prayers not to be lonely affairs, isolated and cut off from the chorus of others. Lead me to prayers that others have left behind, that I find in so praying new and wider possibilities for my own prayers. Help me join my voice in the continual and eternal chorus of praise made by your followers. Amen.

May my lips overflow with praise,
*   for you teach me your decrees.*
May my tongue sing of your word,
*   for all your commands are righteous....*
I long for your salvation, O LORD,
*   and your law is my delight.*

—PSALM 119:171–172,174

13

THE POWER OF SHARED PRAYER

A soul which remains alone…is like a burning coal which
is left by itself: It will grow colder rather than hotter.

—JOHN OF THE CROSS

If two lie down together, they will keep warm.
But how can one keep warm alone?

—ECCLESIASTES 4:11

Several years ago a friend invited me to join him for a hike in a
bird and wildlife sanctuary on the gulf coast of Texas. At first,
as we walked the gravel road that crisscrossed the marshland of the
refuge, I saw only clear sky, clumps of dry reeds, and a few ducks.

I wasn't impressed.

But my friend Merle knew birds. "Look—there!" he would say,
pointing to the sweeping wings of a great blue heron in flight or a
soaring black-shouldered kite. With the help of Merle's sharp eyes and
binoculars, I soon glimpsed roseate spoonbills with broad beaks and
bony legs preening in a distant pond. Merle pointed out every kind
of duck imaginable, more than I could ever name or now remember.
Once he cocked his ear and had me listen for the rasping, eerie call of
grackles perched nearby. With Merle along, a new world opened to
my senses.

Experiences like these remind me that I cannot live well without help. All of us have had friends, mentors, or guides whose influence lives on inside us. Here or there a parent, an aunt, a minister, a schoolteacher, or a neighbor left an indelible mark on our souls. We could not go far without them, without their presence or insight or encouragement or tough words.

It is the same with prayer.

Through the years I have found other *people* indispensable to my growth in praying. They have helped me see glimmers of God's presence I would have overlooked when left to my own devices. They have showed me new angles on what God was doing in my life. They have reminded me to listen to God's truth when I grow complacent or full of myself. Sometimes they have simply stood by me when I knew I should pray but didn't feel like it.

While much of this book has focused on individual, personal prayer, I would be remiss if I did not say that prayer is very much a shared enterprise. It is preeminently done in the company of others. Prayer takes place on many a lonely hillside or empty church building, of course, but especially where, as Jesus said, "two or three are gathered" in his name. Even when we pray in our closets or out on an unaccompanied walk, we do it with and through the support of others. The road to spiritual maturity is more easily traveled with a fellow spiritual pilgrim. Our praying can go only so far if we do not join it with the longing chorus of a worshiping congregation and with companions who walk alongside us.

Knowing that we need other people to pray well, however, may leave us with mixed feelings. We have much to overcome before we turn to others to join with us in prayer. Our culture's love of rugged individualism has so infected our praying that we hesitate. Prayer for many of us still seems like a private enterprise. "We would prefer," writes Eugene Peterson, "to stand tall and alone in our prayers."[1] But "doing it my way" is no mark of heroism when it comes to the spiritual life. Rugged individualism, which whispers to us that only the weak and wimpy need others, is a peculiarly American heresy. Spirituality is not a spiritual do-it-yourself project. We were made for others in life and love, and we were made to be with others when we pray. So we turn now to look at the corporate dimension of prayer. How can the presence and insights of others help us in our praying?

We Can Expect to Find Support from the Presence of Others Who Share Our Spiritual Hungers

Knowing that I do not face the battles of daily life and spiritual growth alone matters a great deal. I cringe to think of the shambles my prayer life would resemble without the wisdom and reinforcement of others.

For a number of years, until a move to another state brought things to a halt, I met for an hour a week, over lunch, with a colleague and friend. We saw ourselves as "mutual mentors." And while the topics of our conversations ranged far and wide, much of what we were about was spiritual growth. Kevin had no license in counseling; I had no certification in formal "spiritual direction," but we brought to each other a simple willingness to listen to the other's joys and struggles and, toward the end of each hour, pray aloud for each other. My praying received over those years countless gestures of encouragement. My times of spiritual dryness or struggle with God met with an understanding presence. Sometimes, when my own praying seemed flat and drained of power, I knew I could count on Kevin's promise to pray. He found himself relying on me in a similar way. What Kevin and I forged now seems unique.

We can find support from others in many settings. Public worship services, house-church meetings, small-group gatherings, Sunday-school classes, even conversation with a neighbor or relative—all of these can provide us an opportunity to know that when we kneel or stand or bow before God, our bent knees and lifted hands and lowered heads are part of a larger whole. We realize that we are not alone when we voice our laments or praises or supplications. We become part of a mighty host, a throng of like-minded believers.

We Can Expect Others to Help Us Make Holy Sense of Everyday Life

I sometimes am tempted to think that my anxiety about paying the bills or being a good father has little to do with more "lofty" concerns, with truly spiritual matters. But I have come to see that from the moment the alarm jars me awake in the morning until the house grows quiet at night, God remains at work in my life—in the dramatic and the ordinary. Spiritual mentors and companions can help me remember to stay alert and open-eyed.

Once a friend and colleague stung me with what I'm sure he felt was helpful honesty. He told me that he found me "naive." I was confused and angry and a little hurt. When my friend and mutual mentor, Kevin, and I got together, I shared what had happened. I knew I needed another perspective, a second opinion, to help me sort through what was true insight and what was simply insult. Kevin listened prayerfully, prayed aloud for me, and offered his perspective. "I think you should ignore the criticism," he said. "I know you, and I think what he is putting you down for is really a God-given simplicity. Don't let go of that." With Kevin's support and spiritual perspective, I was able to move through a difficult and troubling experience.

Sometimes I am liable not so much to miss what God is saying as to misread it. How spiritual some of my ambitions sometimes seem! And how theologically correct my excuses for not doing good. Until, that is, another voice—a minister or neighbor or spouse with the same commitment to Christ—has the courage to point out my mixed motives. When my schedule crowds out time for exercise, family relationships, or prayer, I need someone to remind me that the tasks that seem so urgent may not be worth the compromise. I need others to ensure that my spiritual life does not become an exercise in spiritual self-indulgence.

We Can Expect the Insights of Other Believers to Help Keep Our Praying on Track

Prayer does not automatically confer goodness. It does not even guarantee that we will continue moving closer to truth. It is possible to pray in a way that only immerses us further in pride and self-absorption. Praying can even reinforce our error and arrogance; it simply gives us a spiritual veneer to cover the cracks beneath the surface. And because we tend to see ourselves as more spiritual when we pray, we can become impervious to correction. Wise spiritual teachers know that our own opinions are often deceptive guides.

"He becomes the disciple of a fool who sets himself up to be his own teacher," wrote Bernard of Clairvaux in the twelfth century. Left only to ourselves, we can bend and distort and remake prayer into something that serves our hankerings for self-indulgence. Centuries before Bernard, Augustine wrote, "No one can walk without a guide." Whatever age we live in, to truly grow in prayer requires some un learning and leaving behind.

Indeed, in the spiritual realm we will come across paths that, while attractive at first glance, are not only unhelpful but also dangerous. If, as the Bible says, Satan himself can masquerade as an "angel of light" (2 Corinthians 11:14), we dare not be smug. We do well not to insist that we can always figure things out on our own. Evil almost never looks nefarious at first glance. It is too seductive. We are too willing to be duped. We need the trusted wisdom of theologically sound teachers and guides who are not given to flying after the trendy or silly or shallow. We need companions who are soaked in the wisdom of Scripture, focused on Christ, rooted in the tradition of the church. Which is why the revealed truth of Scripture, sometimes in the words of another human, is so essential. To pray, in other words, requires us to find guidance from others.

Of course, a group, even one that is dedicated to nurturing spiritual growth, can itself become ingrown and prey to spiritual eccentricity. Many of the heresies and horrors of the church's history started among inspired compatriots. "Sometimes," writes Eugene Peterson, "a group diminishes us: we are leveled down, lumped into the less-than-average, and become less than ourselves."[2] We can be led astray by others, not just by our own hearts.

In spite of these risks, so much can happen when we tap into the corporate wisdom and enabling energies of a group. We are more likely to stay focused on truth if we keep our growth in talking to God a cooperative venture. "As iron sharpens iron," the proverb goes, "so one [person] sharpens another" (Proverbs 27:17). How often I have felt myself growing sluggish in devotion only to have my passion rekindled by a sermon or a worship service or a simple word of encouragement from another believer.

Over the years I have discerned within myself a tendency toward perfectionism. My striving to always do everything "just so" has not only brought extra pressures to my relationships but has also colored my image of God. Once when I was bemoaning my failure to be more consistent in prayer, my spiritual mentor at the time gently suggested that I was perhaps too hard on myself when it came to prayer, that I needed to relax more in God's presence and simply enjoy him.

As comforting and reassuring as that message could have been, I resisted. I preferred to see myself as a spiritual athlete, frustrated but determined in my pursuit of devotional heroics. But when, just a short time later, another friend suggested that I needed to rest more in God's promise of acceptance, to receive what God wanted to do in me as a gift, not a merit badge, I found it increasingly difficult to deny what my mentor had said. For all my protests, the remarks I had greeted with skepticism helped bring perspective.

A fellowship group or friend can also shed light on the content of our praying. We may get bogged down in one way or pattern. Perhaps we always concentrate on answers to personal, daily needs. Or perhaps we *never* do. As we have seen, our devotional lives need to include praise to God, confession of sin, intercession for ourselves and others, and thanksgiving for blessings received. We need times of talking to God as well as stretches of restful listening. Another person "listening in" on our praying or reminding us in a teaching of the rudiments of prayer, may steer us back again.

Turning to Another Can Help Us When We Need to Confess

Though I believe we need no mediator between us and God save his Son (see 1 Timothy 2:5), sometimes others can embody God's forgiveness. We may benefit by hearing God's pardon on the lips of another.

I am fascinated by research that shows that unburdening ourselves of painful memories or guilty secrets may significantly improve our physical health. Researcher James Pennebaker demonstrated measurable physiological differences in people who confessed wrongs or talked about disturbing personal episodes compared with those who never divulged their darkest secrets. The difference seemed related not to any specific counsel given in response but rather to the simple act of bringing out into the open what had been hidden.[3]

Confessors can do us good, which may be why, for centuries, indigenous people of North and South America have had elaborate confession rituals wherein tribe members disclosed their wrongdoing to others. It's also why some churches formalize a process by which a person confesses his or her sins to a priest or minister. Whatever the form, the idea is not to carry our burdens alone.

Participation in a Community of Faith and Belief Helps Us Ground Our Spiritual Lives in Something More Solid Than Opinions or Feelings

If we wait only for personal inspiration, our praying will be erratic. We will experience dry spells when we grow in prayer only through the structure of weekly worship, through the support of a group that holds us accountable, and through the honesty of a friend who calls forth the best from us when we are tempted to live off yesterday's spiritual leftovers.

When we pray, we often do so because something inside prompts us to. But we also often pray not only because our feelings nudge us but because we are part of a larger community. When we worship with others, it is not our experience that precipitates prayer. We don't orchestrate it; we participate in it. We are freed from the incessant need to always have to figure out what to say or how long to say it or in what tone of voice. Someone else, vested with the authority (formal or otherwise) of centuries-old tradition, jump-starts our efforts to reach out to God, even providing us the mold into which our words can comfortably, gently fit. Our egos get out of the way. We allow ourselves to relax and be led. We don't have to perform. All our energies become freed; we allow our own prayers, stumbling and faltering as they may sometimes be, to be carried along by something that demands, at least for a time, little from us. The book of Ecclesiastes states that

> Two are better than one,
>> because they have a good return for their work:
> If one falls down,
>> his friend can help him up.
> But pity the man who falls
>> and has no one to help him up! (4:9-10)

PRAYERS

Lord, I'm tempted sometimes to go inside myself. I think I can make my spiritual life a do-it-yourself project. But you have said in your Word that two are better than one, that Jesus is present where two or three are gathered in his name. May my life with you find a dwelling amid a community of friends. Help me find partners and mentors who can encourage my faith and to whom I can give as well. Lead me to those with whom I can join arms and find new strength to move forward. Amen.

Here we are, you and I, and I hope a third, Christ, is in our midst.

—AELRED OF RIEVAULX, *Spiritual Friendship*

PRAYING ON ORDINARY DAYS

On one level, we may be thinking, discussing, seeing, cal-
culating, meeting all the demands of external affairs. But
deep within, behind the scenes, at a profounder level, we
may also be in prayer and adoration, song and worship and
a gentle receptiveness to divine breathings.

—THOMAS KELLY, *A Testament of Devotion*

The time of business does not with me differ from the
time of prayer; and in the noise and clatter of my kitchen,
while several persons are at the same time calling for different things, I possess God in as great tranquility as if I were
upon my knees at the blessed sacrament.

—BROTHER LAWRENCE,
The Practice of the Presence of God

Once a friend who works with prison inmates invited me to
come along. Getting into the prison compound was no easy
matter. We had to pass through a tall fence topped with concertina
coils of barbed wire. Once inside the building, we stepped through a
succession of steel-barred doors, each opened electronically by a bar-
ricaded guard.

When I first saw the inmates, they were filing into a cavernous
dining hall for lunch. Surrounded by the prison's metal grays and dull

olive green walls, wearing standard-issue white uniforms, the inmates stood in a line that snaked down the corridor.

But the inmates who had gathered in the visitors' room were hungry for our company. According to prison policy the visit had to be transacted across a wire-screened counter that separated visitors from inmates. We were one of the inmates' few links with the "outside world," and no direct contact was possible.

But I will never forget what happened toward the end of our time together. Two of the inmates agreed to sing a black gospel song a cappella. Out of the cool barrenness of the prison walls suddenly arose their smooth harmony and floating melody. The inmates' lonely monotony could not stop them from soulfully repeating the refrain, "I went to church last night, and somethin' got a hold of me." It was breathtaking. I had not expected them to lead *me* into God's presence.

But I have been surprised again and again. I begin a day expecting the "same old, same old," only to have my heart suddenly leap at the thought that God is already busy. Or several urgent pastoral needs will call me to drop everything and respond immediately, but instead of feeling panic, I sense a steady, unflappable Presence buoying me up. Or a wave of compassion for someone I'm spending time with will well up from somewhere. The low grind of routine becomes infused with a beauty and power that I could not manufacture on my own. I even find myself humming under my breath, singing hymns of praise in very ordinary places.

⁂

I find that my everyday routine provides perfect opportunities to "practice the presence of God." It's tempting to think sometimes that I would be more spiritual living in a cabin, far from the harried and hurried pace of life. Many of us picture monks and nuns, sequestered from the pressures of what we call "the real world." Or volunteers who live on the grounds of a Christian conference center or church camp. If only we lived there, *then* we could focus on prayer, we think.

I do not doubt that some are called to a life of solitude or radically intentional community, but I also know that most of us live in a world in which colicky newborns keep parents awake through the night, a world of gridlocked traffic and demanding colleagues. It is here, in the stresses of earning a living and trying to get along with the in-laws, that most of us carry out our spiritual lives.

Everyday life is the only setting most of us have in which to grow into a life of prayer. I find this entry in my journal from the time I worked for a book publishing company: "Getting ready for an important meeting at work today, I spent time ironing a shirt and slacks. I realized I could also *pray* about the day, the meeting, how God might want to use me, so that during those minutes of getting ready, I was preparing both physically and spiritually. As I would put on freshly starched and ironed clothes, so I would clothe myself in spiritual readiness." We can be praying underneath and through our activities, not just apart from them. We find that God's presence can be mediated through daily work, not destroyed by it. Christ himself was a carpenter most of his life; surely he sanctified those decades of labor with loving attention to God.

"I keep myself in His presence," wrote Brother Lawrence, "by simple attentiveness and a loving gaze upon God…or to put it more clearly, an habitual, silent and secret conversation of the soul with God…. My most usual method is this simple attentiveness and this loving gaze upon God."[1] A friend once told me how she practices this kind of attentiveness as she works with elderly patients who have senile dementia: "When I am walking from room to room in the nursing home where I work and see someone and stop to interact, my internal voice is praying, 'Give me your love to show this person' or 'Loan me your patience, Lord.' In the times when I am not interacting with anyone, but simply walking, I can go inside [myself] a bit and seek the active, living presence of God."

People such as my friend discover how we do not need to wait until we're retired to get up early enough to read verses from the Bible. We do not have to go on month-long retreats in order to pause in the middle of a day for a few moments of prayer. For most of us, making more room for the spiritual life is not a matter of changing our daily lives but of reorienting our hearts. Growing in prayer is simply a matter of cultivating the garden plot we already have. "Walk and talk and work and laugh with your friends," wrote Thomas Kelly. "But behind the scenes, keep up the life of simple prayer and inward worship. Keep it up throughout the day. Let inward prayer be your last act before you fall asleep and the first act when you awake. And in time you will find as did Brother Lawrence, that 'those who have the gale of the Holy Spirit go forward even in sleep.'"[2]

❖

This practice of an everyday spirituality can move forward in some very simple ways. When activities and pressures lure me into forgetting this spiritual resolve, I find help in little devices. On my bathroom mirror, for example, I have taped an index card with the names of family members, friends, colleagues, and other people who need prayer. The card is so obvious that I see the names whenever I shave, and I'm reminded to mention them in prayer. Even brushing my teeth provides an opportunity to be aware of God's presence. A friend of mine writes the name of someone she wants to pray for on a slip of paper and puts it in her coin purse. Each time she reaches into her purse, she is reminded to pray.

Taped on my bathroom mirror is a note from a friend who, not long ago, was praying for my writing of this book. One morning she felt the Lord give her a distinct message: "Tell him it will go well. My hand is on this." She wrote it on a slip of paper. That little note, a divine communiqué to me during the long hours of writing, has continued to remind me that I am not alone, that all (thankfully!) does not hinge on my abilities.

I also try to turn downtime into time for prayer. I use some of my morning drive time to pray for the people I will visit in the hospital, for the sermon I will write, for the meetings I will need to attend. Each morning as I enter my office, I make turning on my computer and desk lamp an occasion to remember that God is in control of my day. Or on my way home, when I cannot stop the day's events from swirling inside, I don't just relive the things I couldn't get done; I try to gather all those thoughts and scenes into prayers. I carry my day into my praying.

And I carry my praying into my day. I try to take prayerful walks. I savor a cup of tea and thank God for his goodness to me. When I jog in the morning, I take little cards with Scripture verses printed on them for meditation and memorizing. And I let music usher me into the presence of God—Bach, bluegrass, gospel. Martin Marty calls this "hitchhiking," using the books and art forms and expressions of others to help us express devotion to God.[3]

⊹⊱◈⊰⊹

If God shows up in the ordinary turns and straight stretches of life, as I believe he does, it behooves us not to turn aside. We learn to allow God to stand our souls at attention wherever we are. To do that we need to cultivate the ability to see and sense him.

Part of this for me means learning to be more spiritually present wherever I find myself. I am too often not "there" when God does act or speak. I am indeed, as Henri Nouwen once wrote, *pre*-occupied, occupying and packing full my time and space before I get to where I am going, rather than living in the moment. Often that also keeps me from experiencing God. I want to be alert. I want to be open, not oblivious. People who have "abandoned themselves to God," as Jean-Pierre de Caussade wrote,

always lead mysterious lives and receive from him exceptional
and miraculous gifts by means of the most ordinary, natural
and chance experiences in which there appears to be nothing
unusual. The simplest sermon, the most banal conversations,
the least erudite books become a source of knowledge and wisdom to these souls by virtue of God's purpose. This is why
they carefully pick up the crumbs which clever minds tread
under foot, for to them everything is precious and a source
of enrichment.[4]

Once I was visiting a neighbor, William. On his wall I saw a print
of Vincent van Gogh's famous painting of a vase with sunflowers.
There was no mistaking the vivid palette and bold brush strokes.
William told me a story about the painting. "A few years ago my doctor told me I was suffering macular degeneration and that I would
slowly go blind." At the time I visited William, his eyesight was
indeed very dim. When he heard the terrible diagnosis, he immediately bought a ticket to Amsterdam. For a week he did nothing but
make his way through the Van Gogh Museum, slowly soaking up the
beauty and power of the paintings. He wanted to fill his mind with
the images of a master.

Never will I forget the story of a man who concentrated all his
sight on what was beautiful and lasting.

Something in the holy women and men of God throughout history drove them to keep their eyes peeled. They stayed alert and
attuned, even as they led active, fruitful lives. They conditioned their
souls to recognize the holy and heavenly so that they did not miss it.
Their lives were shot through with the presence of God, pervaded
with the fragrance of grace. "Through some moment of beauty or
pain," writes Frederick Buechner, "some sudden turning of our lives,
through some horror of the twelve o'clock news, some dream,…we
catch a glimmer at least of what the saints are blinded by. Only then,
unlike the saints,…we tend to go on as though nothing has hap-

pened. To go on as though something *has* happened is to enter that dimension of life that religion is a word for."[5] "To go on" is to turn toward God and *pray*.

You've heard the adage, seeing is believing. Yet Jesus told one of his disciples, "Blessed are those who have not seen and yet have believed" (John 20:29). We get closed in sometimes, convinced that what we see and experience now is the best we can hope for. We stop expecting much. We grind through one more task, dutifully showing up with an "I've been this way before" written across our faces.

Yet God has resources up his sleeve that we are barely aware of and only rarely glimpse. He can do things we cannot even imagine. Expecting to meet a God of unlimited resources and creativity— believing it before we see it—prepares us to catch his surprising interventions.

A university teacher once told me of a day when a new student came into her office and she struggled with her reaction to him:

> He was huge and his mouth was sort of gaping open, which, combined with his weight, made him look dumb. I looked at his transcript—all Ds and Fs. As I despaired over where to start with this guy, it occurred to me that this might be a good time to pray. I thought to use my customary simple prayer, "Holy Lord, be with me now." I soon felt myself looking deeply into his eyes and *loving* this student. I realized I was in the presence of God—that God was in him, in me, in the room, and in our being together. I was filled with the most wonderful feeling of joy and serenity.

Life, more than we realize, is saturated with the miraculous. I know people who have been healed dramatically, amazingly, when God chose to do so. I have heard so many stories of medical conditions vanishing that I cannot discount them or explain them away.

But I also believe that many miracles escape our notice because we do not have eyes to see them. "Miracles," wrote novelist Willa Cather in *Death Comes for the Archbishop,* "seem to me to rest not so much upon faces or voices or healing power coming suddenly near to us from afar off, but upon our perceptions being made finer, so that for a moment our eyes can see and our ears can hear what is there about us always."[6]

⟡

It's almost comical, the scene that New Testament writer Luke paints in one of his accounts. Jesus has just climbed a mountain to pray, when, as his disciples watch, "his face changed, and his clothes became as bright as a flash of lightning" (Luke 9:29). And the disciples *fall asleep.* Faced with the radiance of the splendor of God, they rub their eyes and stifle a few yawns. Ushered into the jolting presence of God, they curl up for a nap. But sleep here, as in other places in the Bible, represents more than a physical state. Sleepiness is a spiritual condition.

Too often I am plagued by a lack of wakefulness that keeps me from seeing or hearing. A lack of alertness makes me miss the significance of small and great happenings. I sometimes enter prayer with a yawn that says, "I really don't expect much out of this."

But by the grace of God, there are other times. Times when I really smell the freshness of the earth outside my window after a rain. Times when my daughter wanders into my study while I'm writing, and I notice her—really *see* her—for the first time in days. Times when I walk under a starlit sky and know that the One who displays his handiwork in the heavens brings his infinite creativity into my life as well.

I want more and more to stay open to the eloquence and beauty and poignancy of God, who is present in everyday life. If we're willing, God will crack open our heavy-lidded eyes to see things we would surely otherwise miss. The God who never slumbers or sleeps (see

Psalm 121:4) will keep us from snoring our way through the wonder and adventure of living with him.

Once, as I drove to work, I began to feel rising bitterness toward a colleague, someone I would work with that day. This person had snubbed me in the past; she had been condescending, even nasty. My anger at her pettiness was already building. I was rehearsing in my mind how I could slight her in our meeting, be cool and distant in personal contact. But as I prayed, I began to see the possibility—even the summons—for another way of responding. I could be bigger than all this. I saw as I prayed that a person with God's intentions at heart would overcome unpleasantness with good, not with more bitterness.

What a difference that made! I was cordial from the moment I bumped into her in the parking lot. And she, too, was warm this time. I felt reconciliation taking place. A mundane, ordinary day was transfigured. Prayer had injected a new element into a day-in, day-out relationship. God had made a difference.

If "the heavens are telling the glory of God" (Psalm 19:1, NRSV), as the psalmist sang, God save us from slumber. There is too much to see, to notice, to know, for us to spend our lives sleepy or unaware. Whether through a spine-tingling healing or more quiet evidence of the slow work of God, prayer can condition us to be more awake, more alert.

PRAYERS

Lord, if it is you who speak, I want to have ears to hear. Draw my soul from its restless wandering after falsely comforting words. Give me the grace of a quiet heart that I may discern your gentle voice right in the middle of life's daily particulars. Amen.

—◦≡◉≡◦—

Teach me, my God and King,
In all things thee to see,
and what I do in anything
To do it as for thee.

—George Herbert

15

LETTING GO

Whenever you pray, you profess that you are not God and
that you wouldn't want to be, that you haven't reached
your goal yet, and that you never will reach it in this life,
that you must constantly stretch out your hands and wait
again for the gift which gives new life.

——Henri Nouwen, *With Open Hands*

While he strips of everything the souls who give themselves
absolutely to him, God gives them something which takes
the place of all: his love.

——Jean-Pierre de Caussade

It has been a struggle," begins an entry in my journal from years ago.
"I worry endlessly about job opportunities, the move to Indiana,
selling our house. But most of all I wrestle with my career."

A lot was happening in my life. As I prayed, talked with others,
and daydreamed, I had begun to sense a shift in my vocation: a call
to writing and editing. I was honestly perplexed. I had had no jour-
nalism training in college. I had done some freelance writing, but not
enough to launch a career. And at thirty-one I could hardly think
about returning to college; I had to provide for a family, and I owned
a house a crashing real-estate market wouldn't let me sell.

But my worries turned into prayers as my journal entry continued:

"All I can do, Lord, is wait and allow you to fit all the pieces together. Help me to know that you are working everything out according to your will. Use today to allow me to believe again in your goodness." In the entries for the days and months that followed, I often came to God with my hands figuratively clenched with worry, only to feel them gently opening. In prayer I was able to let go, to give up my worries and anxieties to God.

On the morning I penned that journal entry, I could never have foreseen what would happen. Within months I was offered a half-time job—writing a college centennial history. I also found a part-time position at a church in our new location. I had no trouble getting freelance writing assignments. And when the college history book was done, a national magazine offered me a full-time job as an editor. Years later, book contracts allowed me to devote much of my work hours to writing. The opportunities that opened up far exceeded what I could have ever made happen on my own.

But the story didn't end there. I experienced, after years of editing and writing, a sense that God was calling me to return to parish ministry. I began a process that led to yet another vocational bend in the road. There were graduate-school classes to take to become knowledgeable in the history and worship of my new denominational home, a process that, since I was enrolled anyway, ended with my completing a second master's degree. At the outset I had no idea how involved the process would be, nor could I foresee how financially demanding. Most of the time during those months of transition, I had to trust that a guiding hand would bring a good conclusion to my second midstream turn. I had to consciously yield to purposes beyond my own. But the way opened up. Good things happened as a result of that obedience—and they continue to happen.

Although the prayer of relinquishment, as some call it, may come only after long struggle, I have found it to be an essential part of the spiritual life. It could seem, on the surface, like a dreary activity. The language of giving up does not come easily to our lips. And sometimes it *is* an exercise in sheer trust to submit to God. But I have consistently found that surrender and self-abandonment lead to moments of great spiritual progress.

⁘❖⁘

Relinquishment begins with acknowledging that much in life lies beyond our control. We set our goals and make our plans, but who can be sure of the outcome? Who can guarantee that our projects and programs will work tomorrow—or that we will even *have* tomorrow? Permeating all of life is a certain fragility. Of course, much of the time we would prefer to organize and orchestrate. We are drawn to magazine articles with titles like "How to Get What You Want and Protect What You Have." Financial planners pitch their services with tag lines like "Take control of your financial future." But when we maintain our plans and feel in control of our future, we lull ourselves into forgetting that we cannot make the sun rise. We forget that, in the words of the psalm, "this is the day *the LORD* has made," not us (118:24, emphasis added).

Sometimes tragedy gives us our first real reckoning with our need to depend on Another. It can wake us up to the reality of our lack of control. Suffering causes a kind of upheaval in our routine. It leaves us with pain we do not want and loss we would do anything to avoid. We may rebel, we may rage, but we cannot undo what has happened. At such times we see, perhaps more clearly than at any other time, our powerlessness. To be sure, we are called to do many things—vigorously—in most arenas of life; passivity is no virtue. But letting go is, in a real sense, seeing what *is:* We are only a small part of a whole. Our plans are not everything. Even our routine is vulnerable to forces beyond our control.

This truth hits many people hard at midlife. "I woke up one morning," writes one executive, "and realized I was never going to make a million dollars, my marriage was never going to meet my wildest expectations, my children were grown and didn't need me any-more—and this was going to be all there was."[1] We see that not all our ambitions are reachable. Our talents are finite. Opportunities do not come in endless supply. Such moments jar us awake to the fact that we cannot "have it all," that we cannot go on with life as usual and never give an inch.

"Unless a kernel of wheat falls to the ground and dies," said Jesus, "it remains only a single seed. But if it dies, it produces many seeds. The man who loves his life will lose it, while the man who hates his life in this world will keep it for eternal life" (John 12:24-25). Only by dying to the life we know do we find real life. And relinquishment is a kind of dying: to our illusion of self-mastery, to our insistence that we always "do it my way." Perhaps that is what Søren Kierkegaard meant when he said, "God creates everything out of nothing—and everything which God is to use he first reduces to nothing."[2] We need a certain humility and vulnerability for God to use us.

At such times we find ourselves ready to go beyond "my will be done" to "your will be done." We pray that God will make us open to the ways he wants to shape and mold us. We picture ourselves not as finished vases but as clay in the Potter's hands. This shift in our pray-ing may appear so dramatic that it feels like conversion, a radical reorientation of our minds, hearts, wills, and souls. Or, in Thomas Merton's memorable words, we "turn the face of our inner self entirely in His direction," perhaps for the first time.[3]

❖

As we pray with relinquishment, we will discover how much our lives fill with wants and wishes. We set our hearts on a job opening. We hope for a higher salary. We want our children to choose to go to col-lege. We ask for healing.

These and many other wants tumble out in our petitions. That is as it should be. If our desires belong anywhere, it is in prayer. But we can voice our wants in more than one way. We can pray by insisting on a certain thing, concluding that we will find security only if God gives us what we want. But we thereby lose sight of other options, that there can even *be* other options.

There is another way. While we say, "Lord, this is what I want," we do not get too tied to the final answer. Contemplative writer Macrina Wiederkehr makes an interesting distinction along these lines. Rather than pray *for* the things she needs, she has begun to pray *about* them. "When I pray *for* something," she writes, "my prayer tends to be much more narrow. I put expectations on God. I expect something definite to happen and I am disappointed if it doesn't happen.... But when I pray *about* something I am putting expectations on myself. I focus on the presence of God in my specific problem and we look at it together, God and I."[4] We want what we ask for, of course; we pray with faith, believing, but we acknowledge that the One who hears will do good no matter what transpires. Our prayer is directed not so much to the gift as to the Giver. We face into God not just with desire but with open-ended trust. Not only with longing but also with hope.

Until recently my friend Jan worked as an editor in a Midwest town. A harassing neighbor in her apartment building drove her to live in a motel for several weeks while she searched for another place she could afford. "But I kept running up against closed doors," she wrote me. "So I finally realized that instead of presenting God with three options I could live with, I needed to ask God what *he* wanted me to do. I got to the point where I was able to say to God, 'Whatever.'" That became her prayer of relinquishment.

It also became the turning point. Through a series of events she sees as providential, she was offered a position at a spiritual retreat house in another state, a job that combines her skills and background in ways that still leave her amazed. She did not get what she first wanted—no apartment turned up. But she met the Answerer. And he gave her something else. Something even better.

Prayers of relinquishment are powerful because they give God more space in which to move and act. They do not obliterate our wills; they transform them, or at least temper them. They serve as a kind of invitation for God's power and presence. Macrina Wiederkehr writes,

> What God most longs to discover in us is our willingness
> to embrace ourselves as we were at our beginning—empty,
> little, and poor. Our willingness gives God free space within
> us to work out the Divine Plan. Our potential for greatness
> is tremendous. Acceptance of our littleness makes it possible
> for our greatness to emerge. Our littleness is not a choice. It
> is simply the way we are. Our greatness, however, is a choice.
> When we choose to accept the life God has given to us,
> when we allow God to fill our emptiness, we are choosing
> greatness.[5]

We see this in Paul the apostle. He struggled with God, three times pleading that God remove a "thorn in [the] flesh"—some illness or chronic condition. The Lord came back each time with only the promise that "my grace is sufficient for you, for my power is made perfect in weakness" (2 Corinthians 12:7-9). But what a power it was! Paul never was healed, and he had to relinquish that hope, but God worked through Paul with astonishing power. Paul's relinquishment became a time not of defeat but of opening to the One who has ultimate power over any obstacle. An ability beyond human reckoning was released. In losing our lives, we find them (see Mark 8:35). By giving up, we gain far more than we would ever possess on our own.

It is not hard to see, then, that relinquishment is not the same as resignation. We are not talking about a droopy, "I couldn't care less what happens" outlook. "Resignation," as writer Catherine Marshall notes, "lies down in the dust of a godless universe and steels itself for the worst."[6] Relinquishment, on the other hand, says, "I choose to believe that God has a solution." One response grows out of depression and lack of belief. The other takes the moment at hand and marries it to hope.

Think of a garden scene in what is perhaps history's best-known example of relinquishment: Jesus on the night before his death by crucifixion. We see him in the Garden of Gethsemane praying to his Father, "Take this cup from me. Yet not what I will, but what you will" (Mark 14:36). But *before* that poignant acceptance of God's purposes, he prays, "*Abba,* Father,…everything is possible for you" (verse 36). It was his conviction that God was *Abba* that allowed him to merge his purposes into God's. It was not sheer determination, but a conviction that a caring, fatherlike God held all possibilities in his hands. If the worst happened, even then God would work out some good thing. Jesus's crucifixion would have a resurrection attached to it.

I am told that our English phrase *self-surrender,* which has overtones of defeat and grudging submission, has a different sense in the French language. *Se livrer* means "to hand over or deliver oneself to" in a freely chosen act of love. "To surrender" in this sense "is a total turning to God in self-giving, a response to a gesture of love."[7]

Relinquishment, then, is not leaping into some vast cosmic unknown. It is becoming willing to be led by a Good Shepherd. It is to hold lightly our lives, which were first given by a God of love. When we pray "your kingdom come," we are not stumbling along with a God of chance or caprice. We are submitting to a God who has plans of good for us, not evil. "God's gifts put man's best dreams to shame," wrote poet Elizabeth Barrett Browning. He has resources and plans that would boggle our imaginations.

Yes, this approach feels risky sometimes. But why let our fear of what we cannot see keep us from giving ourselves to the One who sees all?

✦

Some years ago, to pastor Dale Galloway's great grief, his wife asked for a divorce. "Many times as a minister," he wrote, "I have heard people talk like they thought there were some things worse than death. At that moment and in the following days for me, life was worse than death." But then, at the end of his rope, he offered a prayer of relinquishment.

> I practiced what I call "let go and let God." I took my hands and cupped them in front of me, held them up, and verbally put inside those hands everything I was fretting over and didn't have any answer to. I said out loud as I held up both hands, "There it is, God; I can't change it, I don't know what to do with it, it's all so unacceptable to me. I have been fighting it. I just don't know what to do. There it is, Lord, I give it all to you. I give to you what people think about me." As I talked to God, I turned my hands upside down and said, "There it is, Lord. It's all yours." As I stretched my fingers out as far as I could, turning my hands upside down so that it was impossible to hold on to anything, as I dropped my arms to my side, a wonderful feeling of serenity suddenly spread throughout my entire being. I now had peace in the midst of the storm.[8]

This morning as I prayed—thinking about the day ahead of writing, pulling together a sermon, family responsibilities, house chores—I prayed, "I give you my life, Lord. Please take it and use me." There were no crashing cymbals in the air above me. I felt no jolts of electricity. But what I said had huge import. I made myself available to a great Love and Power. In a kind of self-emptying, I made myself available to be filled.

Our prayers of release and acceptance need not be elaborate. We need not worry much about the words. More than anything, a prayer of letting go means coming into God's presence with our agendas quieted. It means reverently opening our lives and hearts to a God of infinite possibilities.

Many times as I pray such prayers, I find it helpful to gently hold my hands open, palms upward. The customary prayer posture in the first decades of the church's life, scholars tell us, was different from what we have learned during childhood table graces. Rather than sitting hunched over with hands clasped together, people prayed with open hands and outstretched arms.

I like that picture of openness. It helps in praying to unclasp my hands and release my heart to the surprises God wants to work. I expect God to reveal more and use me more as I loosen my grip and relax my control.

My relinquishment is not always perfect, of course. Sometimes my surrender of self is partial. And many times during the course of a day, I take back my life and try to make things turn out as I want. But God can use even my imperfect offerings of self. He has gotten used to my occasional reservations and protests. Intention is what matters, not perfection. God, from whom all that is good comes, will take my simple offering and carry forward his plans and purposes.

I am trying to discover the art of relinquishing more of my life to God. As I walk through the scenes of my busy, filled schedule, I can consciously make room for the One who can make all the difference. It can be as simple as a murmured, "I have faith in you, Lord." Or as direct as asking, in dependence, for his help. Saying such prayers can help us get ourselves out of the way and give God room to move.

I know relinquishing prayer will not always be easy. I will no doubt cling to new schemes and prospects that at the time seem too good to let go of. But I am learning that by releasing, I receive. In letting go I am held safe. So I trust God to help me find the courage to release my grip.

Prayers

Father, it often seems easier to hold the reins of my life tightly. I think I want to control and manage and manipulate. But in my wiser moments I know that you alone know what is best. Help me to want you and your will more than anything else. Amen.

⊷═◉═⊶

Forth in your name, O Lord, I go,
My daily labor to pursue,
You, only you, resolved to know
In all I think, or speak or do.

—Charles Wesley

MOVING FORWARD

Our pursuit of God is successful just because he is
forever seeking to manifest himself to us.

—A. W. TOZER

The Living Christ within us is the initiator and we are the
responders. God the Lover, the accuser, the revealer of light
and darkness presses within us. "Behold I stand at the door
and knock." And all our apparent initiative is already a
response.

—THOMAS KELLY, *A Testament of Devotion*

Because I just missed making it to my father's hospital bedside
before he died, he and I never got the chance to do some important talking. As I mentioned before, I had things to say, emotional
closure I wanted to bring. And I had questions to ask. I knew very
little about his financial affairs, nothing about provisions he made for
Mother.

Later that evening, back at my parents' Santa Monica home, I
began going through Dad's papers and records. I didn't know what to
expect. Fortunately most of the bills, canceled checks, and passbooks
were in one place—a closet next to my old bedroom, which Dad had
turned into his home office. To my surprise, I also found a copy of the

family will, which I had never seen and heard him mention only in passing. I trembled inwardly as I opened it. There had been those few years of strain in our relationship, even a time when I was ostracized. Would I be mentioned? It was not the money I cared about, but my status.

But there was my name—even my children's! He had decreed to me a full share of the inheritance. I grieved his passing, sorrowed not to have bid a final farewell, but at least I knew my standing. There was no lingering question about how he saw me.

We have similar fears, perhaps not always rational, about our relationship with God. Can we always count on his loving us and walking with us? When we rail at him or feel his absence, can we keep going in trust?

With questions like these in the background, I want to explore how prayer fits in the deep corners of our hearts. How does it become an ongoing part of our lives? To do so, it helps me to think of growth in prayer in terms of three metaphors: a gift, a journey, and an adventure.

Growth in Prayer Is a Gift

Often in this book I have looked at *how* we pray. I have tried to be intensely practical about what we do. But much of what happens when we pray has to do with intangibles. And much of our experience of prayer comes from outside of us, from God's side of the equation. This is not to say that we become passive, only that we don't feel it all depends on us. Spirituality is not a decathlon in which sheer grit and buckets of perspiration determine the final outcome. It is not a declaration of independence. Nor is it tied to some religious "talent" or innate spiritual genius.

A relationship with God is instead something we receive, not something we achieve. It is not a reward but a gift. It is not something we earn but something we are given. And just as our salvation begins with letting go of all the accomplishments we think make us presentable to God, so does our growth in the Spirit. We come not pushing, but letting ourselves be pulled.

Prayer has mostly to do with God—his grace, his willingness, his invitation. What we say in our devotional times is our response. Prayer is our answering more than it is our initiating or inventing. In prayer we may knock on the door, but we do so having been invited to come in the first place. In fact, we can say that in Jesus Christ, God opened the door of possibility of communion with him in the first place. In prayer we begin to walk through.

A radio talk-show host once interviewed me on the topic of angels. I will never forget the plaintive remarks of one call-in listener. She confessed to having difficulty in praying. "But what I do," she said, "is just give my prayers to my angels and let them carry my requests up to God." This listener believed that God was aloof and inaccessible. But because God himself invites us to pray, because he does not reside in a far-off heavenly realm, we do not need to turn to celestial stand-ins or reconcile ourselves to a distant deity. God is actually eager to hear our prayers. That is the generosity that can be ours in Jesus Christ.

Other religious traditions have a different take on prayer. They tend to say that we pray to get through to God. Making connection with the Absolute is our job, and an arduous (or dicey) one at that. But Jesus demonstrated that the point is not that we find God but that he has found us. We don't pray to reach out as much as to reply. Salvation, the Bible's word for our rescue from our prisons of self and sin, is not our doing, but God's. We accept what God has done. That is what the coming of Jesus means. That is the good news of Christianity. That is the good news about prayer.

Vincent Donovan lived for a time in Tanzania, teaching and preaching among the Masai people. One day he was talking with a Masai elder about the struggles of believing in God. The elder was pointing out that the word Vincent had come up with to translate the word *faith* was not very satisfactory. In this case, the word meant only "to agree to."

> He said to believe like that was similar to a white hunter shooting an animal with his gun from a great distance. Only his eyes and his fingers took part in the act. We should find another word. He said for a man really to believe is like a lion going after its prey.... His legs give him the speed to catch it. All the power of his body is involved in the terrible death leap and single blow to the neck with the front paw, the blow that actually kills. And as the animal goes down the lion envelops it in his arms,...pulls it to himself, and makes it part of himself. This is the way a lion kills. This is the way a man believes....
>
> But my wise old teacher was not finished yet.
>
> "We did not search you out, Padri," he said to me. "We did not even want you to come to us.... You followed us away from your house into the bush, into the plains, into the steppes where our cattle are,...into our villages, into our homes. You told us of the High God, how we must search for him,... We have not left our land. We have not searched for him.... He has searched *us* out and found us. All the time we think we are the lion. In the end, the lion is God."[1]

For centuries Christian theologians have debated the meaning of Jesus's death on the cross. Their theories of the Atonement certainly shed light on this centerpiece of Christian faith. But consider this bare-bones summary: The Cross means that intimacy with God is wildly, wonderfully possible. The guilt and shame and frustration that sometimes make prayer seem out of reach need not make us halt or hover. God will not allow a breakdown in fellowship with him to be the last word. He comes among us in and through his own Son to restore what has been broken and devastated. Finally we are freed from the burden of living moral, spiritual lives in order to be saved.

We experience Christ's salvation power so that we *can* live the lives God intends. We simply ask God to make it so. We ask him to make what Christ did real for our lives.

"He bore with us," wrote an anonymous third-century writer, "and in pity [God] took upon himself and gave his own Son as a ransom for us—the Holy for the wicked, the Sinless for sinners, the Just for the unjust, the Incorrupt for the corrupt, the Immortal for the mortal.... O sweet exchange!... O benefits unhoped for!"[2]

This giftlike quality is not just for our beginnings in prayer. We stay open to the way God "gifts" our praying throughout all of life, knowing that beyond our efforts will always be possibilities we could never have dreamed of. We come expectantly. That means the spiritual life will sometimes surprise us. We may trudge through months—or even years—when little seems to happen. Other times we will find ourselves intoxicated by God. The Bible, after all, speaks of forty-day wilderness fasts and temptations in one breath, and being drunk with the Holy Spirit in the next.

I have already talked about the dry times. So in this chapter I want to talk about the times when prayer "takes off." Here, for example, is a quiet Quaker scholar, Thomas Kelly, who decades ago penned a spiritual classic called *A Testament of Devotion*:

> There come times when prayer pours forth in volumes and originality such as we cannot create. It rolls through us like a mighty tide. Our prayers are mingled with a vaster Word, a Word that at one time was made flesh. We pray, and yet it is not we who pray, but a Greater who prays in us. Something of our punctiform selfhood is weakened, but never lost. All we can say is, Prayer is taking place, and I am given to be in the orbit.[3]

Or here is John Cassian, a monk from centuries ago, describing what he calls the "prayer of fire":

That ineffable prayer which rises above human consciousness, with no voice sounding, no tongue moving, no words uttered. The soul lights up with heavenly illumination and no longer employs constricted, human speech. All sensibility is gathered together and, as though from some very abundant source, the soul breaks forth richly, bursts out unspeakably to God, and in the tiniest instant it pours out so much more than the soul can either describe or remember when it returns to itself.[4]

We cannot force such moments. But we can wait. We can prepare the ground. And then from time to time, quite often when we least expect it, God will give our prayers flight. What had been a discipline becomes an art. Our stumbling words are lifted into song. We "pray in the Spirit" (Ephesians 6:18), to use Paul the apostle's phrase, lofted above the normal constraints.

"I play in a symphony orchestra," one Internet friend of mine writes. "There are times when the entire group of eighty musicians becomes inspired—we don't know why—and we play absolutely magnificently. We all say, 'What happened?' No one can answer. It happens in the spiritual life also."

It happens in my praying sometimes. My heart pours forth its longings without faltering. Or I feel an overflowing love for God that needs no scripting. My normal speech seems so limited that I pray in unknown tongues, the sounds and syllables streaming out in effortless stirring.

I can only call those moments gifts, foretastes of the communion we will enjoy in heaven.

Growth in Prayer Is a Journey

One of the biblical tradition's rich images for life with God is that of a path or road. We follow a way. People who pray are more like pilgrims than settlers. There is always something more God leads us to.

We pitch a tent every now and then, but do not settle for good. People who pray are more like pioneers than settlers.

Do we never stop on this path? Are we always seeking God? In one sense our search is over; for in our seeking we have been found. God has met us and made us his own. The Bible uses the wonderful, reassuring language of family: We are children of a loving Father. Whether the image is of having been born anew or adopted (see Ephesians 1:5), we have an irrevocable place in God's family. No wall or abyss jeopardizes that communion.

But in another sense the searching and seeking never end. Always growth and deepening will continue.

So it is that the Bible shifts metaphors from parent and child to husband and wife: God is "married" to his people. Christ is a bride; his church, the bridegroom. The kingdom of God is a marriage supper. If a human marriage relationship can deepen and become richer through a lifetime, how much more can a relationship with a God of inexhaustible love! The first taste of intimacy, the first discovery of God's wondrous presence, is followed by another. And another. And on it goes. To find that we can talk to God is the mere starting point. We are lured on to experience more and more of the ineffable joys of being filled with God. Our search for greater intimacy with him is never finished, and it grows more thrilling the further we proceed.

I remember once mentioning spiritual restlessness in a positive way to a friend. He was taken aback. He thought that since he had committed his life to God, his restlessness would forever cease. For him a restless heart meant agitated bewilderment. I tried to help him reclaim the holy value of restlessness. Touched by God's love, we will always long for his embrace. When we see the Beautiful, we are never satisfied with just a glimpse. When we taste God's sweetness, we will find our spiritual hunger deepening. We will want more, and that will lead us forward. "You called and cried out loud," wrote Augustine, "and shattered my deafness. You were radiant and resplendent, you put to flight my blindness. You were fragrant, and I drew in my breath and now pant after you. I tasted you, and I feel but hunger and thirst for you. You touched me, and I am set on fire to attain the peace which is yours."[5]

Growth in Prayer Is an Adventure

I sometimes forget, but experience after experience reminds me that life with God is beyond my predicting or imagining. It can never be reduced to the tidy or known. The dictionary definition of *adventure* spells out what we know intuitively about prayer: It is a bold and usually risky undertaking.

I read recently about a book with an intriguing title: *The Courage to Pray.* Someone was commenting on how the title struck him, how he has prayed about having courage for a number of things, but courage *to pray? How intriguing,* he thought. And the more I think about it, the more sense it makes. What if the untamable God we approach (and assume we know) turns our conceptions of prayer upside down? If prayer puts us in relationship with God, who can guarantee that we won't be changed by the encounter? So something in us wants to hold back from intimacy with God, from all the unpredictability of its potential power.

"I've been praying for you," my friend Steve Brown once wrote me. "But if things get too bad, let me know, and I'll let up." To say that God will not leave us alone has two meanings: (1) He will not leave us stranded, and (2) he will not leave us the same. When we follow, we can expect him to lead us to places we would never have gone on our own.

We can also expect times when we do not know what is next. One day some years ago, I set out on my regular jogging route. Because of the dense morning fog, I could barely make out turns in the path ahead. Only by recognizing wayside bushes and fences and other markers could I keep my feet on the trail that finally led home. In my life with God, I usually see only a few curves and turns in front of me. I follow One whose ways are beyond imagining. Who can say where God will take me?

> Oh, the depth of the riches of the wisdom and knowledge of God!
>> How unsearchable his judgments,
>> and his paths beyond tracing out! (Romans 11:33)

Which is why another definition of *adventure*—"an exciting undertaking"—also fits. Precisely because God is beyond our predicting, prayer will not be boring. As the title of a book by a friend says, prayer is *Living by God's Surprises.*[6] We think we want to be in control, to be safe. But in our deeper selves, we want something more than comfort. We want Someone larger than ourselves to lift our lives out of the ordinary and ordered.

⊰❖⊱

In the first book of C. S. Lewis's fanciful Chronicles of Narnia, Mr. Beaver tries to describe to the children Aslan, the lion, the Christ-figure who is wild and free and comes at will.

> "I tell you he is the King of the wood and the son of the great Emperor-Beyond-the-Sea. Don't you know who is the King of Beasts? Aslan is a lion—*the* Lion, the great Lion"
>
> "Ooh!" said Susan. "I'd thought he was a man. Is he—quite safe? I shall feel rather nervous about meeting a lion."
>
> "That you will, dearie, and no mistake," said Mrs. Beaver, "if there's anyone who can appear before Aslan without their knees knocking, they're either braver than most or else just silly."
>
> "Then he isn't safe?"
>
> "Safe?" said Mr. Beaver. "Don't you hear what Mrs. Beaver

tells you? Who said anything about safe? 'Course he isn't safe. But he's good. He's the King, I tell you."

"I'm longing to see him," said Peter, "even if I do feel frightened when it comes to the point."[7]

God, the awe-inspiring, frightening, but gracious King, leads us into adventure. We pray and can never know for certain precisely where the answers will lead. We cannot guarantee that prayer is a safe act.

But I keep praying. Some mornings I manage little better than a groggy, distracted few minutes. Other times I'm moved almost to tears. One week I may not feel much of anything. Then one day a glimpse of God's fiery power leaves me elated. The constant is God. And usually, when I sense him, I cannot help wanting to be with him. And sensing that he stands listening, I cannot help talking to him.

PRAYER

Lord, your Word says,
  "No eye has seen,
    no ear has heard,
  no mind has conceived
    what God has prepared for those who love him."
Help me in all my days to at least glimpse the wonders of your goodness and mercy.
  Amen.

Appendix

A STUDY GUIDE ON PRAYER

For many of us, few areas in life inspire more resolutions—or create more guilt—than prayer. "I know I should pray, and I want to," a friend confesses, "but it's a struggle." Reading a book on prayer, such as this one, may create in you a new eagerness or expectancy. It may also leave you wondering how to delve deeper and further explore honest questions.

This desire to grow in prayer is age-old. One of Jesus's disciples came up to his master and exclaimed, "Lord, teach us to pray" (Luke 11:1). The disciples had already prayed for years, having grown up in households in which prayer was taught and modeled. Synagogue services and training in the Hebrew Scriptures would have left them with much knowledge. Still, they sensed something different about the way Jesus talked with his Father. They saw a depth and reality in his relationship with God that made them restless for something more. Jesus was happy to show them a better way.

Scripture is filled with guidance for praying. Its many-splendored teachings and model prayers can enrich your times with God. They can turn your perhaps sputtering resolutions into times of intimacy and fruitfulness, your sometimes stuttering words into language rich with communion. As you make your way through this study, let your prayer be that of the disciple who came to Jesus, anxious to learn. And let your heart be open to God's instruction and guidance in the Bible, for he is eager to teach you and lead you into new and deeper experiences.

Study 1
Corresponds with the Introduction and Chapter 1 in Text

HOW SHALL WE COME?

Read Luke 18:9-14; Hebrews 4:14-16

The introduction states, "Talking to God is more art than science. It does not require technique as much as relationship. It has more to do with will than skill. Conversation with God involves our deepest selves and our most everyday moments."

Perhaps you read that as a freeing invitation to pray, or to pray more. But you may wonder about the proper approach to God.

A friend described how, as a child, she was so afraid when she thought of God that she would hide under a box. Growing up in a household filled with abuse and hurtful words, she feared God as Someone who would punish her—or at least not like having her around. That view changed as she grew older and grew in knowledge of God, but in a vivid way, that childhood experience makes us ask, What is our appropriate posture as we come to God?

As you will soon see, the two Scripture passages in this study seem to contradict each other. One suggests that we can only approach God humbly, with deference and reverence. The other instructs us to come confidently, knowing we are loved. How do these contrasting passages fit together?

The answer has to do with perspective. Because of who we are, we can never come into God's presence proudly demanding that he do our bidding. Instead, we remember that "all have sinned and fall short of the glory of God" (Romans 3:23). That includes us! And so we come to prayer depending on God's mercy.

But because of who *God* is, we do not shrink back in fear. God's compassion will not allow him to turn a deaf ear to our cries. His love is the ground on which we can confidently stand whenever we approach him.

Consider the following questions as you continue to ponder this happy tension between humility before God and confidence in prayer.

1. Do you come easily to prayer? When have you needed courage to speak to God?

READ LUKE 18:9-14.

2. Jesus had a target audience for this parable. To whom did he address it, and why is this significant (see especially verses 9 and 11)?

3. There are two people in Jesus's parable: a Pharisee and a tax collector. What did these titles tell Jesus's listeners about each person? (*Hint:* One title meant esteem; the other invited disdain.)

4. Despite the Pharisee's righteous actions—"I fast twice a week and give a tenth of all I get" (verse 12)—why was God not pleased with him? In what way do we see in him a prideful distortion of the assurance we can rightly enjoy?

5. We sense the tax collector's discomfort at being in the temple. What do you think brought him there? Was it in part the kind of spiritual hunger mentioned in the introduction? (Reread the first paragraph in the introduction, which declares, "Prayer is capturing our imaginations like never before.")

6. What does it mean to be "justified before God" (verse 14)? (See also Romans 3:23-28 and 5:1-2.)

7. In what ways does the example of the tax collector challenge you in your practice of prayer? What about his humility before God serves as an example to you? How might it give you new hope that God will hear your prayers?

Read Hebrews 4:14-16.

8. Name two things Jesus does as high priest. (See also Hebrews 5:1-10; 7:23-25; 9:24-28; and 10:11-22. In these scriptures we find Christ as both a mediator between God and humans and a sacrifice for our sins.)

9. Because of Jesus, what can we expect to receive from God?

10. What is the connection between the invitation to "approach the throne of grace with confidence" (verse 16) and the parable's rebuke of the Pharisee's confidence?

11. Psalm 24:3-4 admonishes that only he who has "clean hands and a pure heart" should come into God's presence. Have you ever felt that you were not good enough to talk with God? Explain your answer.

12. How can prayer be a time to *receive* something, not just say something? What do you expect God to give you when you pray?

Study 2
Corresponds with Chapters 4 and 6 in Text

GREAT IS THE LORD!

Psalm 145; 1 Thessalonians 5:16-18

Chapter 6 quotes the question from the Westminster catechism (a catechism is an older and organized way to train people in the Christian faith). The question is, "What is the chief end of humankind?" The answer, learned by those being taught the faith, is, "To glorify God and *enjoy* him forever."

To glorify God is to give God glory, that is, to honor him as *glorious*. It is to fill our prayers with joyous remembrances of his goodness. In the New Testament alone, the passages that urge or describe praise and thanksgiving to God number well over two hundred. And the words themselves take on astonishing variety; in addition to *glorify* are *bless, thank, worship, magnify, extol*—to name just a few. Then we uncover the rich vocabulary of praise in the Old Testament. The psalm for this study is a fine example.

As we move closer to God's presence, grateful praise saturates our hearts. This "attitude of gratitude" establishes a mature and exciting foundation for our prayer life.

1. Why do you pray? What do you hope to accomplish? In what way do you see prayer as a way to give God the honor and glory that is due him?

READ PSALM 145:1-2,21.

2. These verses frame the psalm. Make a list of the verbs used in these verses and define each of them.

3. What is the psalmist praising God for in these verses? What does the psalmist's use of extremes ("for ever and ever," "every," and so on) teach us about God's worthiness and our responsibility?

READ PSALM 145:3-7.

4. What is it about God that makes him worthy of praise?

5. Again, note the verbs ("commend," "tell," "proclaim"). How can our praises teach our children—our own or others'—about God?

6. What are some of God's "mighty acts" and "awesome works" that we can commend to our children?

7. Verse 7 speaks of celebrating God's goodness and singing of his righteousness. How can this verse help us incorporate praise into our times of worship church?

READ PSALM 145:8-20.

8. List some of the characteristics of God for which we might praise him.

9. According to verses 11 and 12, praise has a role in evangelism, that is, in telling others the good news of God. What might that role be?

10. Some writers suggest that praise, which typically concentrates on God and his wonderful nature, differs some from thanksgiving, which may tend to focus more on expressing gratitude for actual gifts or good circumstances. In what ways is that a helpful distinction for your own praying? In what ways does it not always fit, in that the two sometimes naturally intertwine?

READ 1 THESSALONIANS 5:16-18.

11. Do you experience constant joy in your life? If so, where does it come from? If not, do you find this admonition a simple reminder to count your blessings or an unrealistic and burdensome expectation? Explain.

12. Think over the schedule of an average day in your life. Where could you fit prayer and thanksgiving into your day?

13. Why do being joyful, praying continually, and giving thanks in all circumstances fit together into God's will for us? How can prayer, especially thankful prayer, make us joyful?

Study 3

Corresponds with Chapter 5 in Text

A CRY FOR FORGIVENESS

1 John 1:8-10; Psalm 51

Consider Jennifer, mentioned in chapter 5: "Because divorce loomed, and her upbringing made her see divorce as almost unforgivable, Jennifer felt she was angering God. Guilt consumed her. She stopped praying. 'I'm afraid that God won't hear my prayer. I feel unworthy, and it's driving me further from God.' Far from feeling oblivious to guilt, she was paralyzed by it."

Or consider some of the other responses mentioned in the first section of the chapter that attest to the reality that we sometimes do wrong.

We can count on the fact that in our fallenness we will sometimes fail. Can we depend just as certainly on God's promise to forgive?

1. How did you feel as a child when you realized you had done something your parents wouldn't like? When, if ever, have you experienced that feeling as an adult?

READ 1 JOHN 1:8-10.

2. How do you understand this passage as it relates to Jesus's words in Matthew 5:48: "Be perfect, therefore, as your heavenly Father is perfect"? (*Note:* Some commentators argue that the word *perfect* in Matthew 5:48 suggests completeness or maturity, not absolute moral spotlessness.)

3. If we say we do not sin, we actually do two things. What are they?

4. What happens when we confess our sins? How can this knowledge free you when you approach God's throne in prayer? (See also Hebrews 4:14-16, which suggests that our having been forgiven helps us come boldly to God.)

READ PSALM 51:1-6.

5. What characteristics of God make confession inviting?

6. What must occur in us before we are willing to confess our wrongdoing?

7. When we do something to injure or upset another person, why would we confess that to God? According to verse 4, against whom have we sinned in addition to the person we harmed or failed?

8. What did Jesus's death and resurrection accomplish for us in our dilemma of being "sinful at birth" (verse 5)? (Paul addresses this question in Romans 5:12-19.)

READ PSALM 51:7-12.

9. Note the anxiety expressed here by the "sinner." What does unconfessed sin do to our relationship with God? In what ways can our not owning up to our sins and misjudgments leave us feeling distant from God?

10. Sin made the psalmist feel unclean. How does he describe the experience of forgiveness for which he longs? If you can, describe a time you felt this way after confessing prayer.

READ PSALM 51:13-19.

11. For the psalmist, forgiveness brings an eager desire to tell people about God. Discuss how our experience of sin, confession, and God's consequent forgiveness can play a role in bringing others to Christ.

12. Have you made confession a regular part of your prayer time? Why or why not? What would be the value in doing so?

A LISTENING HEART

John 10:1-5; 1 Samuel 3:1-21

T he first epigraph for chapter 9 is a quote from C. S. Lewis:

> The moment you wake up each morning…all your wishes
> and hopes for the day rush at you like wild animals. And
> the first job each morning consists in shoving them all back;
> in listening to that other voice, taking that other point of
> view, letting that other, larger, stronger, quieter life come
> flowing in.

Sometimes in our desire to do prayer well, we may forget that prayer is more than talking. Faithful praying often involves a leisurely sense of quiet. We may "accomplish" much in our praying by simply waiting in the Lord's presence for his comfort, insight, or guiding word.

Despite our hurried, harried lifestyle, Psalm 46:10 reminds us to pause long enough to consider the Lord: "Be still, and know that I am God." Fruitful prayer relies not just on an active mind or busy tongue but on a quiet heart that listens for God.

1. Consider a time when you needed to know God's will concerning a decision you faced. How did you attempt to discover God's will? Do you feel that you ever did?

READ JOHN 10:1-5.

2. How does the shepherd in this parable lead his sheep?

3. The watchman (verse 3) apparently oversees an area where several flocks are penned. Which sheep does the shepherd call to follow him when he comes into the pen?

4. How are the sheep able to recognize the shepherd's voice (see John 10:14)? What do they do when they hear the voice of a stranger?

5. Jesus likened himself to the shepherd (see John 10:11). Who, then, do the sheep represent? (See also Psalm 23, Isaiah 40:11, and Jeremiah 31:10.)

6. In what ways does Jesus call or speak to us? How can we tell his voice from that of a stranger who would pretend to be him or call us to follow other leaders in different directions?

READ 1 SAMUEL 3:1-21.

7. How does the writer of 1 Samuel describe the times during which the boy Samuel lived?

8. Notice how long it took Eli to recognize that it was God who called Samuel. In what way might his slowness be related to the description of the times in verse 1? What part might his own sinfulness play in his slow recognition of God's voice?

9. Why did Samuel not recognize God's voice? (Might it, for example, have to do with his youth and his need for a

mature guide?) What role did Eli play in Samuel's life at this point?

10. Note that God did not relay his message until Samuel showed himself ready to listen. What might that suggest to us about our prayers? How can silence—a receptive, listening silence—become an appropriate part of prayer in your life?

11. What is the significance of verse 18? Would Samuel have trusted his vision without Eli's confirmation? Why or why not?

12. How do today's times compare with those described in verse 1? What challenges do you face in light of what chapter 3 of the book calls "noisy, harried times"? How does God communicate with us today? In what ways can we listen and respond to him?

DON'T BE AFRAID TO ASK

James 5:13-18; Luke 11:9-13

Prayer is sometimes just a matter of asking. "Often it is the simple, repetitious phrases that our Father in heaven finds most irresistible," said sixth-century writer John Climacus. Referring to characters mentioned in the Gospels, he continued, "One phrase on the lips of the tax collector was enough to win God's mercy; one humble request made with faith was enough to save the good thief."

Scripture teaches us that God delights to hear us—always. He offers us a standing invitation. "Come, all you who are thirsty," he said through his prophet (Isaiah 55:1). "Ask...seek...knock," said Jesus to his disciples (Luke 11:9). "In everything," said Paul the apostle, "present your requests to God (Philippians 4:6)."

1. What happens when you receive a gift from someone? Do you feel obligated to return the favor?

READ JAMES 5:13-18.

2. According to these verses, when should we pray?

3. What is a "prayer offered in faith" (verse 15)?

4. Why was Jesus's prayer in Gethsemane (see Mark 14:36; Luke 22:42) a "prayer offered in faith"? How can you pray with this kind of faith in your own circumstances?

5. Do these verses suggest that God's answers to our prayers are limited by our righteousness (verse 16) or our earnestness (verse 17)? Consider Luke 17:6 as you explain your answer.

6. Note the promises in verses 15 and 16: Prayer "will make the sick person well"; "he will be forgiven"; pray for one another so that "you may be healed." On what are these promises based?

7. Who is "a righteous man," and how well does the word *righteous* describe you? What could make your prayers more "powerful and effective"?

READ LUKE 11:9-13.

8. List the three verbs mentioned in this passage. What result does Jesus say each will produce?

9. Can we take verse 10 literally? If we ask God for something—anything—will we get it, or will we find limits to God's generosity? Consider John 14:14: "You may ask me for anything *in my name,* and I will do it." In what ways will asking in Jesus's name affect what we ask for?

The phrase "in Jesus's name" implies something about the character and nature of the One through whom we pray. How might awareness of Christ's character actually shape the prayers we say?

10. Who do you think Jesus meant when he said "everyone" (verse 10)? Did he mean "every person" or "everyone who is a disciple" or "everyone who comes in faith" or something else? Explain your answer.

11. What did Jesus mean when he said, "Knock and the door will be opened to you"? Consider verse 13. What is Jesus urging us to seek?

12. Do you sometimes feel self-centered in asking God for what you personally need? Do you try to lay your own concerns aside when you pray, fearing they may be trivial? Consider the following quote from C. S. Lewis and try to put it into practice this week:

> We must lay before [God] what is in us, not what ought to be in us.... It may be that the desire can be laid before God only as a sin to be repented; but one of the best ways of learning this is to lay it before God.... If we lay all the cards on the table, God will help us to moderate the excesses.... Those who have not learned to ask Him for childish things will have less readiness to ask Him for great ones. (C. S. Lewis, *Letters to Malcolm: Chiefly on Prayer*)

Study 6

Corresponds with Chapters 7 and 14 in Text

PRAYERS FOR THE KINGDOM

Ephesians 6:18-20; 1 Timothy 2:1-7

One of the privileges of prayer is interceding for the spread of God's good work in the world. In such praying we take particular people, specific situations, our churches—even whole nations—to God. We invite him to intervene and carry out his will. This may mean praying for missionaries who are carrying the gospel to the far corners of the earth or praying for a ministry to the homeless in our own community. It may mean praying for hurting people we do not know or asking God to help those we know intimately who need hope.

We sometimes forget how significant such praying can be. "More things are wrought by prayer than this world dreams of," wrote the poet Alfred Lord Tennyson.

Jesus had such praying in mind when he urged us to pray, "Your kingdom come" (Matthew 6:10). The writer of Psalm 67 had it in mind when he prayed, "That your ways may be known on earth, your salvation among all nations" (verse 2). And in this study the apostle Paul tells us even more about the importance of prayer for the advance of God's kingdom.

1. When you're reading the newspaper or watching the news on television, do you ever feel moved to pray for someone mentioned there? If so, share some specific examples and how you prayed.

READ EPHESIANS 6:18-20.

2. What does Paul mean when he tells us to "pray in the Spirit" (verse 18)? (You might check various translations to find what shades of meaning the phrase has.)

3. Name all the kinds of prayer you can think of. How can we use the many varieties of prayer to make certain we "pray...on all occasions" (verse 18)?

4. Paul urged his readers to "be alert" in their praying and instructed them to "always keep on praying" (verse 18). Why does there seem to be a sense of urgency in Paul's words? (*Note:* Also look at Ephesians 6:11-13.)

5. Paul tells us to pray "for all the saints" (verse 18). The term *saint* in the New Testament refers not to an especially holy person but to all believers in Christ. Using verses 19 and 20, how can you pray for pastors, missionaries, people in your church, and other Christians?

6. What did the apostle Paul want the Ephesians to specifically pray for him? Verse 20 discloses that Paul was writing from prison—why did he not ask them to pray for his release?

7. Think of someone you know whose prayer request might be similar to Paul's—"that I may declare [the gospel] fearlessly, as I should" (verse 20). When will you plan time in your daily schedule to pray for him or her?

READ 1 TIMOTHY 2:1-7.

8. To whom does the "everyone" in verse 1 refer? What do prayers have to do with "all men" being saved (verse 4)?

9. Verse 2 singles out "kings and all those in authority" as an important focus for our intercession. What is the promised outcome of our prayers for those in authority?

10. Does it make you uncomfortable to pray for governmental leaders, especially those with whom you disagree? Do you think that prayer for our nation's leaders should be a regular part of church worship services? Why or why not?

11. How might verses 3-6 guide us as we pray for missionaries and the spread of the gospel throughout the world?

12. Besides prayers for the world's spiritual needs, how can we touch the physical world through our requests, our intercessions, and our thanksgiving? Write three sentence prayers that lift to God the world's needs.

13. If you've concluded from this study that you need to give more attention to intercession, in what specific ways can you do so? If you can, list some other areas in which to intercede besides the ones mentioned in this study?

14. Chapter 14 suggests ways to make prayer a more visible and present part of daily life: "When activities and pressures lure me into forgetting this spiritual resolve, I find help in little devices." Examples included placing a card on a bathroom mirror or other prominent place or using a repeated daily action (such as turning on a computer) as a reminder for prayer. What are some ways you might practice prayer through the use of such helps?

WHEN THE DOOR WON'T OPEN

Psalm 13; 2 Corinthians 12:7-10

C hapter 10 suggests several ways to understand unanswered prayer. We may ask ourselves, for example, Have I failed to recognize God's blessings for what they are? Have I not seen that God is working for my best interests through delays in answers to prayer? Or we may ask, Have I failed to distinguish between God's long view and my timing? After all, in our day of instant everything, we may be "quickaholics," as someone aptly put it. "We prefer our answers—perhaps even answers from God—in sound bites."

At the same time, many of us recall situations when what *seemed* so necessary or urgent turned out not to matter. Or we found that the object of our request might have hurt us. God takes the long view, and in his mercy he may say no.

Unanswered prayers can also teach us lessons about about God's dependable care in times of hardship, about our own need to develop character, or about the necessity of persistence in prayer. However, some unanswered requests remain a mystery. For all our praying, waiting, and believing, God sometimes will not answer a prayer that by all accounts looks good. For this reason we may naturally find ourselves at times expressing frustration, even disappointment or anger toward God.

The Bible reassures us that, in an important sense, there is no such thing as unanswered prayer. God may not answer as we expect or want, but he always listens and always responds. And even when our emotions do not seem "presentable," God understands and continues to love us.

1. Recount an incident when you prayed earnestly for something and God seemed not to answer.

READ PSALM 13.

2. According to the psalmist, why had God seemed to not answer his prayers (see verse 1)? In what way did he seem to think that God wouldn't respond?

3. Does the psalmist seem faithless when he accused God of forgetting him and delaying response to his prayers? Why or why not? What does it mean to cry out to God?

4. Jesus urged his followers to be persistent in praying. But what motivates such persistence? What is the role of unanswered prayer in teaching us perseverance?

5. Quickly outline the psalm, noting the progression of the thoughts expressed by the psalmist. How did the very act of praying bring him relief?

READ 2 CORINTHIANS 12:7-10.

6. The apostle Paul suggested an interesting reason why God might allow suffering (verse 9). What is it? When and how has God dealt with you in a similar way?

7. Three times Paul "pleaded with the Lord" to take away the "thorn." What made him willing to plead? Why did he stop pleading after the third time?

8. Paul's prayer did not go unanswered. God simply said no. What did God's answer help Paul understand about himself?

9. In what sense might we say that there is no such thing as unanswered prayer? How can we tell when God is answering our prayer with a no?

10. How is God's power made perfect in weakness? How have you seen this in your life or in the life of someone you know?

11. Tell about a time in your life when God's answer to your prayer seemed delayed. What do you now see as one possible reason God answered with "wait"?

12. What does a child learn about God when his or her earnest prayer for a bike or some other present goes unanswered? How can God use what we perceive to be unanswered prayer to teach us about himself?

Study 8
Corresponds with Chapter 11 in Text

PRAYING THAT JUST WON'T QUIT

Luke 11:5-8; 18:1-8

W/e may find our praying complicated by several things: distractions and a wandering mind, for instance. Even more daunting may be a dimming of our vision of prayer's powerful effects. A weakening of our resolve gets intensified by our instant-gratification culture. We may not be used to persisting at much of anything.

Jesus told a few parables that suggest we may sometimes be polite or lazy to the point of indifference in our praying. Here we learn to keep approaching the Father, even when the answer won't come easily.

1. Tell about someone in your life—a parent, teacher, child, salesperson—who refused to give up in his or her efforts to convince you to be or do something.

READ LUKE 11:5-8.
2. Note that the man in Jesus's parable went to a friend, someone with whom he had already established a relationship. How might the story have been different if he had approached a stranger?

3. What did the man in the parable ask his friend? Was it a reasonable request made under reasonable circumstances? Explain.

4. Notice that in Jesus's time the man could not simply run out to an all-night grocery store or take his guest to a restaurant. How did his need give energy to his request? When in your life has desperation pushed you to keep asking for something?

5. At first the friend refused to help the man, but what made him change his mind?

6. Some versions of the Bible read "because of the man's *persistence*" (verse 8, emphasis added). Others read "*boldness.*" Discuss the passage from the differing perspectives of these two words.

READ LUKE 18:1-5.

7. What was the character of the judge in the parable? Why did he at first refuse to give the widow a just settlement?

8. What caused the judge to change his mind? Did his character change?

READ LUKE 18:6-8.

9. Jesus compared God to the unjust judge and contrasted their characters. How did Jesus say God and the judge were alike? How were they different, and why does this offer us such hope?

10. How does persistent prayer differ from the "babbling" of pagans, who "think they will be heard because of their many words" (Matthew 6:7)? If God knows what we need before we ask him (see Matthew 6:8), why should we "cry out to him day and night" (Luke 18:7)?

11. Jesus closed this lesson on prayer with an unsettling question: "When the Son of Man comes, will he find faith on the earth?" (verse 8). How would you answer him?

12. Have you ever stayed up all night praying for another person or a particular concern? How does the idea of persistent, persevering prayer fit with the common adage, "Let go and let God"?

Study 9
Corresponds with Chapter 12 in Text

PRAYING LIKE JESUS

Matthew 6:9-13

"That we are made to pray," we read in chapter 12, "does not mean we never need 'practice.' Sometimes we need to do more than improvise. Our prayers need sound instruction. When I run low on words…I need teachers. I need to spend time with the prayers of others until I gain a sense of them. Then my own prayers will have greater fluency and depth."

A key resource in learning to pray more profoundly is the most famous and oft-quoted prayer of the Bible, the one Jesus taught his disciples: the Lord's Prayer.

And with good reason. This is far more than a "rote prayer" to be said woodenly or routinely. Here Jesus introduces the great themes of praying: praise, confession, and petition. He reveals the One we address in prayer and shows us what we can appropriately ask for ourselves.

Since in the Lord's Prayer we're repeating the words and themes Jesus himself taught us, we know we're praying at God's invitation—and according to his will.

1. When you pray, how do you begin? How do you know what to include? Think of times your prayers made a good start but then ran aground for lack of clear direction regarding what might come next.

READ MATTHEW 6:9-10.

2. To whom did Jesus address this prayer?

3. How can God be both close ("Our Father") and far off ("in heaven")?

4. What kind of response did Jesus expect when he addressed God as his heavenly Father?

5. Notice that one of the first phrases in this prayer praises God (*hallowed* means "holy, revered"). Why is it important to begin our prayers by acknowledging God's greatness?

6. What pictures come to mind when you hear the word *kingdom?* Is God's kingdom here now, coming in the future, or both? Explain your answer.

READ MATTHEW 6:11-13.

7. What does Jesus tell us we should request for ourselves?

8. How do you typically approach God with your needs (confidently, tentatively, humbly)? Explain your answer.

9. Does Jesus's use of imperative verbs "give us," "forgive us," and "lead us" mean we should demand that God give us what we need? Why or why not?

10. Which lines in the prayer refer to our relationships with others?

11. Why would Jesus link the forgiveness of our sins with our willingness to forgive other people? How have you seen this confirmed as a principle of life?

12. Jesus tells us to regularly pray for deliverance from evil. What does our need for such a prayer demonstrate about our world and ourselves?

13. When you pray, do you ever fear that God may not be listening? If so, why? How can knowing that we are praying in Jesus's own words help us get past our fears and keep on praying?

TWO ARE BETTER THAN ONE

Matthew 18:19-20; Hebrews 10:23-25

A soul which remains alone…is like a burning coal which is left by itself: It will grow colder rather than hotter," said sixteenth-century spiritual writer John of the Cross. Centuries before, the writer of Ecclesiastes observed, "Two are better than one…. If one falls down, his friend can help him up. But pity the man who falls and has no one to help him up! Also, if two lie down together, they will keep warm. But how can one keep warm alone?" (Ecclesiastes 4:9-11).

All of us need others to help us stay spiritually warm. Prayer has an individual aspect, to be sure, but it is never merely private. We may pray in our closet, but we also need to pray with others. Only then will our misconceptions be challenged, our spirits find new strength, and our prayers grow to maturity.

1. Describe a time when the stress or confusion of a situation caused you to seek out another person with whom to pray or to ask others to pray for you.

READ MATTHEW 18:19-20.

2. To whom was Jesus referring when he said "two of you" (verse 19)?

3. What did Jesus promise will happen "if two of you…agree about anything you ask for" (verse 19)?

4. How do you interpret such a sweeping promise? If we pray with another person for something, does this guarantee we will get it?

5. What did Jesus say will happen when "two or three" gather in his name (verse 20)?

6. What is the significance of Jesus's presence during prayer? How does that affect our prayer times together?

7. If you pray regularly with another person or with a group, what benefits have you discovered? If you have not practiced this kind of prayer, whom might you trust to share times with God?

READ HEBREWS 10:23-25.

8. How might we use a prayer time with other Christians to "spur one another on toward love and good deeds" (verse 24)?

9. The Greek word translated "give up" in verse 25 refers to desertion and abandonment. When we "abandon" meeting with one another, what do we lose?

10. A poll several years ago indicated that 70 percent of Americans say that they have many acquaintances but few close friends, and this causes a void in their lives. When have you experienced loneliness in your Christian life? How

could praying with another person offer an antidote to
your loneliness?

11. What might "meeting together" encompass (verse 25)?
Name settings and occasions besides Sunday-morning worship that you have found particularly encouraging. Have
these occasions included prayer?

If you can, this week try calling a friend or a person you respect about
a particular need you have. At the very least, ask him or her to pray
for you during the week. You might also ask that person, or someone
such as a minister or Sunday-school teacher, for a chance to pray *with*
that person.

THE ARSENAL OF PRAYER

Ephesians 6:10-18

To hear some believers talk about the Christian life, you might imagine it's simply a pleasant stroll. But the apostle Paul described it as a battle. He used warfare imagery and spoke of standing ground under the assault of spiritual evil.

Prayer, then, is not always gentleness and peace. Sometimes it feels like a gritty struggle. In Ephesians 6 Paul teaches us how to be soldiers for Christ. He trains us to employ the armor of God as we find strength for the battle in him.

1. Have you ever experienced a time when praying required an intense struggle? What was the nature of the struggle?

READ EPHESIANS 6:10-18.

2. In these verses Paul writes about "our struggle," our need to "be strong in the Lord" and "to stand." What does this suggest about the Christian life?

3. Against whom do we struggle, according to Paul? What examples can you give of this kind of struggle?

4. If our struggles are not against "flesh and blood" (verse 12), how do we develop discernment to see past the human face of evil to the dark power that motivates it?

5. Paul makes it clear that human strength is not sufficient to fight this battle. Mere physical armor cannot protect us or give us the victory. Why?

6. What are the various pieces of the "armor of God" (verse 11) that Paul urges us to don? How does each piece protect us or equip us?

7. What part does prayer play in this spiritual warfare? How do we battle in prayer for someone?

8. One way we stand our ground against evil is to keep ourselves pure and righteous. Paul wrote, "You were once darkness, but now you are light in the Lord. Live as children of light" (Ephesians 5:8). How can prayer help us set "the breastplate of righteousness in place" (verse 14)?

9. How do we take up the "shield of faith" (verse 16)? How can prayer strengthen our faith?

10. Look again at each piece of God's armor. Pray sentence prayers for a specific way you need God to strengthen and protect you in each area.

WHEN WORDS FAIL US

1 Corinthians 2:6-16; Romans 8:26-27

Sometimes, for all our desire to pray, the words don't seem to come. We may not know what to say. We may find words insufficient to articulate all that is within. Our speech may seem a poor vehicle for communication in the presence of an awesome God.

Other times the problem seems to be a lack of progress. We find ourselves facing struggles we thought we had settled months or even years before. Our devotion lags. It is hard to muster much energy or enthusiasm for prayer.

The Bible gives us good news for such times. The Holy Spirit himself, whom Paul said "searches all things, even the deep things of God" (1 Corinithians 2:10) comes to help us in our praying. That means we never pray alone or unaided.

1. Describe a time or two in your life when words have seemed inadequate to express your feelings.

READ 1 CORINTHIANS 2:6-16.
2. Paul speaks of God's "secret wisdom" that no one has seen or heard or even thought of (see verses 7-9). How, then, do we know about it?

3. Who knows God's thoughts (verse 11)? How does Paul conclude we can know God's thoughts (verse 12)?

4. What is the nature of the "spirit of the world" (verse 12)? How does that spirit affect a person's ability to understand the things of God (verse 14)?

5. What does "the Spirit who is from God" do for us (verse 12)?

6. Paul recognized that the message he preached came to him from the Spirit, in words shaped by and given by the Spirit. How does this concept relate to our prayer life?

READ ROMANS 8:26-27.

7. What "weakness" was Paul referring to in verse 26?

8. How does the Spirit help us in our weakness?

9. In 2 Corinthians, Paul wrote about the words the Spirit gives us. In this passage he wrote about "groans that words cannot express" (verse 26). What did he mean? How is human language too limited (too *human*) to express all that the Spirit wants us to pray? How might the Spirit help?

10. Do you turn away in frustration from prayer when you can't seem to find the words? Have you ever asked the Holy Spirit to intercede for you? If so, what was the result?

11. Have you ever awakened from a sound sleep (or a daydream!) sensing that you needed to pray for someone? How do you think the Holy Spirit was involved in this? What happened?

12. Sometimes we can feel a longing to express something to God, but the longing doesn't seem easily put into words. Do we have to use words in order to pray? Why or why not?

13. Think back over the weeks you have been studying prayer. How has your prayer life improved? What can you do to strengthen your communication with God?

STUDY GUIDE REFERENCES

Lewis, C. S. *Letters to Malcolm: Chiefly on Prayer.* New York: Harcourt Brace Jovanovich, 1963.

Life Application Bible. Wheaton, IL: Tyndale, 1988.

Packer, J. I. *I Want to Be a Christian.* Wheaton, IL: Tyndale, 1979.

Reapsome, Martha. *The Journey of a Lifetime.* Wheaton, IL: Harold Shaw, 1993.

Wright, Vinita Hampton, and Carol Plueddemann, comps. *World Shapers.* Wheaton, IL: Harold Shaw, 1991.

NOTES

Foreword

1. J. B. Williams, ed., *The Lives of Philip and Matthew Henry* (Edinburgh, Scotland: Banner of Truth, 1974), 77-78, quoted in N. H. Keeble, *The Literary Culture of Nonconformity* (Leicester, UK: Leicester University Press, 1987), 213.

Introduction: First Steps

1. Kenneth Woodward, "Talking to God," *Newsweek,* January 6, 1992, 39.

2. Anna Quindlen, *One True Thing* (New York: Random House, 1994), 59.

3. Augustine, *Confessions,* trans. Henry Chadwick (Oxford: Oxford University Press, 1991), 3.

4. Anne Lamott, *Traveling Mercies: Some Thoughts on Faith* (New York: Pantheon, 2000), 82.

5. David Jeremiah, *Prayer: The Great Adventure* (Sisters: OR: Multnomah, 1997), quoted in Traci Mullins, ed., *In This Quiet Place: Discovering the Pleasure of Prayer* (Grand Rapids: Zondervan, 1999), 8.

6. Wesley L. Duewel, *Touch the World Through Prayer* (Grand Rapids: Zondervan, 1986), quoted in Mullins, ed., *In This Quiet Place,* 16.

7. John Powell, *He Touched Me: My Pilgrimage of Prayer* (Niles, IL: Argus Communications, 1974), 50.

8. Philip Yancey, *The Jesus I Never Knew* (Grand Rapids: Zondervan, 1995), 165.

9. Henri J. M. Nouwen, *Life of the Beloved: Spiritual Living in a Secular World* (New York: Crossroad, 1992), 37.

Chapter 1: A Cry for Help

1. Dom Chapman, quoted in Richard Foster, *Prayer: Finding the Heart's True Home* (San Francisco: HarperSanFrancisco, 1992), 7.

2. Brother Giles, "The Sayings of Brother Giles," *The Little Flowers of St. Francis,* trans. Raphael Brown (New York: Doubleday, 1958), 278.

3. George MacDonald, quoted in Edythe Draper, *Draper's Book of Quotations for the Christian World* (Wheaton, IL: Tyndale, 1992), 480.

4. Michael Allen, *This Time, This Place* (Indianapolis, IN: Bobbs-Merrill, 1971), 117.

5. Ann Belford Ulanov and Barry Ulanov, *Primary Speech: A Psychology of Prayer* (Atlanta: John Knox, 1982), 15.

Chapter 2: The Simplest Language in the World

1. For this image I am indebted to Henri J. M. Nouwen, *The Way of the Heart* (New York: Ballantine, 1981), 31.

2. Emily Dickinson, quoted in Thomas Becknell, *The Beginning of Wisdom: Prayers for Growth and Understanding,* ed. Mary Ellen Ashcroft (Nashville: Moorings, 1995), 3.

3. Sandra Goodwin Clopine, quoted in Jim Castelli, *How I Pray* (New York: Ballantine, 1994), 21.

4. See Castelli, *How I Pray,* 12.

5. Gerald G. May, *The Awakened Heart: Opening Yourself to the Love You Need* (San Francisco: HarperSanFrancisco, 1991), 60.

6. Quoted in Nouwen, *Way of the Heart,* 64.

7. Thérèse of Lisieux, *Autobiography of St. Thérèse of Lisieux,* trans. Ronald Knox (New York: P. J. Kenedy, 1958), quoted in Sherwood Eliot Wirt, ed., *Spiritual Power* (Westchester, IL: Crossway, 1989), 105.

8. *Midrash Tehillim* 5.6, quoted in James H. Charlesworth, "Jewish Prayers in the Time of Jesus," *The Princeton Seminary Bulletin,* no. 2 (1992): 47.

9. See *Midrash Tehillim* 5.6, quoted in Charlesworth, "Jewish Prayers," 48.

Chapter 3: A Quietness of Soul

1. Richard Foster, *Prayer: Finding the Heart's True Home* (San Francisco: HarperSanFrancisco, 1992), 1.

2. Eudora Welty, quoted in Nicholas Dawidoff, "Only the Typewriter Is Silent," *New York Times,* August 10, 1995.

3. Ladislaus Boros, quoted in Edythe Draper, *Draper's Book of Quotations for the Christian World* (Wheaton, IL: Tyndale, 1992), 563.

4. Cornelius Plantinga Jr., "Background Noise," *Christianity Today,* July 17, 1995, 42.

5. John Edward Southall, quoted in Robert Llewelyn, Kallistos T. Ware, and Mary Clare, *Praying Home: The Contemplative Journey* (Cambridge, MA: Cowley, 1987), 43.

6. Carl Honoré, *In Praise of Slowness: How a Worldwide Movement Is Challenging the Cult of Speed* (San Francisco: HarperSanFrancisco, 2004).

7. For this analogy I am indebted to Thomas Merton, *No Man Is an Island* (New York: Harcourt Brace Jovanovich, 1955), 127.

8. Quoted in Henri J. M. Nouwen, *The Way of the Heart* (New York: Ballantine, 1981), 37-38.

9. Susan Annette Muto, *Pathways of Spiritual Living* (New York: Doubleday, 1984), quoted in Bob Benson Sr. and Michael W. Benson, *Disciplines for the Inner Life* (Nashville: Nelson, 1989), 76.

10. Plantinga, "Background Noise," 42.

11. John of the Cross, quoted in Thomas Dubay, *Fire Within* (San Francisco: Ignatius Press, 1989), 65.

12. Nouwen, *Way of the Heart,* 65.

13. Iris V. Cully, *Education for Spiritual Growth* (San Francisco: Harper & Row, 1978), 54.

14. Quoted in George H. Gallup Jr. and Timothy Jones, *The Saints Among Us* (Harrisburg, PA: Morehouse, 1992), 55.

15. Anthony Bloom, *Beginning to Pray* (New York: Paulist, 1970), 92-94.

Chapter 4: The Way of Intimacy

1. See Morton Hunt, *The Universe Within: A New Science Explores the Human Mind* (New York: Simon & Schuster, 1982), 222-23.
2. Simone Weil, *Waiting for God* (New York: Harper & Row, 1951), 68-69.
3. Weil, *Waiting for God*, 68-69.
4. Robert Coles, *The Spiritual Life of Children* (Boston: Houghton Mifflin, 1990), 40.
5. Bilquis Sheikh, *I Dared to Call Him Father* (Eastbourne, UK: Kingsway, 1979), 51-53, quoted in Roger Pooley and Philip Seddon, *The Lord of the Journey* (London: Collins, 1986), 90-91.
6. Reynolds Price, "The Gospel According to Saint John," *Incarnation: Contemporary Writers on the New Testament*, ed. Alfred D. Corn (New York: Penguin, 1990), 72.
7. See Matthew 6:6-8; 7:7-11; 18:19; 21:22; John 14:13-31; 15:7,16; 16:23-33; James 1:5; 1 John 5:14-15.

Chapter 5: Facing Our Failings

1. Harry Crews, *A Childhood: The Biography of a Place* (New York: HarperCollins, 1983), quoted in Annie Dillard and Cort Conley, eds., *Modern American Memoirs: 1917–1992* (New York: Harper-Collins, 1995), 8-9.
2. Joe Klein, "Lawyering the Truth," *Newsweek*, January 22, 1996, 34.
3. Charles W. Colson, *Born Again* (Grand Rapids: Revell, 1995), 113, 116-17.
4. Shakespeare, *King Lear*, quoted in David Bevington, ed., *Four Great Tragedies: Hamlet, Othello, King Lear, and Macbeth* (New York: Bantam, 1988), 434-35.
5. Kenneth Woodward, "Do We Need Satan?" *Newsweek*, November 13, 1995, 63-64.
6. Elie Wiesel, *All Rivers Run to the Sea: Memoirs* (New York: Knopf, 1995), 77-78.

7. Isaac the Syrian, quoted in Alan E. Nelson, *Broken in the Right Place* (Nashville: Nelson, 1994), 88.

8. Martin Luther, quoted in Roger Pooley and Philip Seddon, eds., *The Lord of the Journey* (London: Collins, 1986), 124.

Chapter 6: Enjoying God

1. Gale D. Webbe, "The Toughest Virtue," *Christianity Today*, November 9, 1984, 82.

2. See Richard L. Pratt Jr., *Pray with Your Eyes Open: Looking at God, Ourselves, and Our Prayers* (Phillipsburg, NJ: Presbyterian and Reformed, 1988), 27.

3. Elizabeth Barrett Browning, *Aurora Leigh*, bk. ix, quoted in Edythe Draper, *Draper's Book of Quotations for the Christian World* (Wheaton, IL: Tyndale, 1992), 97.

4. C. S. Lewis, *Letters to Malcolm: Chiefly on Prayer* (New York: Harcourt Brace Jovanovich, 1964), 90.

5. C. S. Lewis, *Reflections on the Psalms* (New York: Harcourt Brace Jovanovich, 1958), 90-91.

6. Brother Lawrence, *The Practice of the Presence of God* (New York: Doubleday, 1977), 68.

Chapter 7: Not Afraid to Ask

1. Fyodor Dostoyevsky, *The Brothers Karamazov* (New York: The Modern Library, 1959), 40.

2. Sheldon Harnick and Jerry Bock, "If I Were a Rich Man," copyright © 1964, Alley Music and Trio Music.

3. Larry Dossey, *Healing Words: The Power of Prayer and the Practice of Medicine* (San Francisco: HarperSanFrancisco, 1993), 6-7.

4. C. S. Lewis, *Letters to Malcolm: Chiefly on Prayer* (New York: Harcourt Brace Jovanovich, 1963), 19, 20.

5. See Rosemary Ellen Guiley, *The Miracle of Prayer*, ed. Claire Zion (New York: Simon & Schuster, 1995), 217.

6. I am indebted to C. S. Lewis for this image, which, in slightly different form, appeared in *Letters to Malcolm,* 55-56.

7. E. M. Bounds, quoted in Traci Mullins, ed., *In This Quiet Place: Discovering the Pleasure of Prayer* (Grand Rapids: Zondervan, 1999), 42.

8. Ellis Peters, *A Morbid Taste for Bones: A Mediaeval Whodunnit* (New York: Macmillan, 1977), quoted in Madeleine L'Engle, *Two-Part Invention: The Story of a Marriage* (San Francisco: Harper & Row, 1988), 185-86.

Chapter 8: Emotions and Getting Real with God

1. Thomas Merton, *Thoughts in Solitude* (Boston: Shambhala, 1958), 14.

2. Paul Tournier, quoted in Edythe Draper, *Draper's Book of Quotations for the Christian World* (Wheaton, IL: Tyndale, 1992), 481.

3. Elie Wiesel, *All Rivers Run to the Sea: Memoirs* (New York: Knopf, 1995), 84.

4. Richard Foster, *Prayer: Finding the Heart's True Home* (San Francisco: HarperSanFrancisco, 1992), 23.

5. Frank Bianco, *Voices of Silence: Lives of the Trappists Today* (New York: Doubleday, 1991), xi-xx.

6. Bianco, *Voices of Silence,* xi-xx.

Chapter 9: Listening for God

1. Lily Tomlin, quoted in Dallas Willard, *In Search of Guidance: Developing a Conversational Relationship with God* (San Francisco: HarperSanFrancisco, 1993), 6.

2. Frederick Buechner, *The Alphabet of Grace* (San Francisco: HarperSanFrancisco, 1989).

3. W. B. Yeats, "Crazy Jane Talks with the Bishop," in *The Collected Poems of W. B. Yeats,* ed. Richard J. Finneran (New York: Simon & Schuster, 1989).

4. Madeleine L'Engle, *Two-Part Invention: The Story of a Marriage* (San Francisco: Harper & Row, 1988), 123-24.

5. C. S. Lewis, *The Problem of Pain* (New York: Macmillan, 1947), 81.

6. Quoted in Carin Rubenstein, "Your Spiritual Self," *New Woman,*
    March 1995, 86-87.
7. Mother Teresa, quoted in Philip Yancey, *Finding God in Unexpected
    Places* (Nashville: Moorings, 1994), 210.
8. For more information, see Leanne Payne, *Listening Prayer: Learning
    to Hear God's Voice and Keep a Prayer Journal* (Grand Rapids: Baker,
    1994), 26.

Chapter 10: Making Sense of Unanswered Prayers

1. See Roger Steer, *George Müller: Delighted in God* (Wheaton, IL:
    Harold Shaw, 1981), 161.
2. C. S. Lewis, *Letters to Malcolm: Chiefly on Prayer* (New York: Har-
    court Brace Jovanovich, 1963), 59.
3. William Carey, quoted in F. Deaville Walker, *William Carey: Mis-
    sionary Pioneer and Statesman* (England: SCM, 1926), 47; Roger
    Pooley and Philip Seddon, eds., *The Lord of the Journey* (London:
    Collins, 1986), 281.
4. Oliver Sacks, *The Man Who Mistook His Wife for a Hat* (New York:
    Simon & Schuster, 1970), 108-10.
5. Martin Buber, *The Dialogue Between Heaven and Earth,* quoted in
    David Manning White, *Finding God: The Paragon Treasury of Inspi-
    rational Quotations and Spiritual Wisdom,* vol. 2, *Eternal Quest* (New
    York: Paragon House, 1992), 70.
6. C. S. Lewis, *A Grief Observed* (New York: Bantam, 1961), 4-5.

Chapter 11: When Praying Seems Impossible

1. John Donne, *John Donne's Sermons on the Psalms and Gospels,* ed.
    Evelyn M. Simpson (Berkeley and Los Angeles: University of
    California Press, 1967), 226.
2. Tad Dunne, *We Cannot Find Words* (Denville, NJ: Dimension
    Books, 1981), 14-15.
3. Dom John Chapman, *The Spiritual Letters of Dom John Chapman,
    O.S.B.* (London: Sheed and Ward, 1938), 52-53, quoted in Henri

J. M. Nouwen, *The Road to Daybreak: A Spiritual Journey* (New York: Doubleday, 1988), 117.

4. Steve Brown, *Approaching God: How to Pray* (Nashville: Moorings, 1996), 46.

5. George Arthur Buttrick, *Prayer* (New York: Abingdon-Cokesbury, 1942), 263, quoted in Richard Foster, *Prayer: Finding the Heart's True Home* (San Francisco: HarperSanFrancisco, 1992), 17.

6. Thomas Merton, *Thoughts in Solitude* (Boston: Shambhala, 1958), 46.

7. Quoted in George Gallup Jr. and Timothy Jones, *The Saints Among Us* (Harrisburg, PA: Morehouse, 1992), 53.

8. C. S. Lewis, *Mere Christianity* (New York: Macmillan, 1952), 51.

9. David Bolt, quoted in Edythe Draper, *Draper's Book of Quotations for the Christian World* (Wheaton, IL: Tyndale, 1992), 480.

Chapter 12: Discovering Model Prayers

1. Richard Foster, "Growing Edges," *Renovaré Perspective,* October 1996, 1.

2. Eugene Peterson, quoted in Foster, "Growing Edges," 17.

3. Eugene Peterson, quoted in Foster, "Growing Edges," 87.

4. Simon Tugwell, *Prayer: Prayer in Practice,* vol. 2 (Dublin: Veritas, 1974), 62-63, quoted in Roger Pooley and Philip Seddon, eds., *The Lord of the Journey* (London: Collins, 1986), 232.

Chapter 13: The Power of Shared Prayer

1. Eugene H. Peterson, *Answering God* (San Francisco: Harper & Row, 1989), 89.

2. Peterson, *Answering God,* 19.

3. See James W. Pennebaker, *Opening Up: The Healing Power of Confiding in Others* (New York: Avon Books, 1990), 14.

Chapter 14: Praying on Ordinary Days

1. Brother Lawrence, *The Practice of the Presence of God* (New York: Doubleday, 1977), 68-69.

2. Thomas Kelly, *A Testament of Devotion* (New York: Harper & Row, 1941), 39.

3. Martin Marty, quoted in Jim Castelli, ed., *How I Pray* (New York: Ballantine, 1994), 92.

4. Jean-Pierre de Caussade, *The Sacrament of the Present Moment*, trans. Kitty Muggeridge (San Francisco: Harper & Row, 1981), 80.

5. Frederick Buechner, *The Alphabet of Grace* (New York: Walker and Company, 1970), 94-95.

6. Willa Cather, *Death Comes for the Archbishop* (New York: Vintage, 1990), quoted in Dan Wakefield, *Expect a Miracle: The Miraculous Things That Happen to Ordinary People* (San Francisco: HarperSan-Francisco, 1995), 6.

Chapter 15: Letting Go

1. Source unknown.

2. Søren Kierkegaard, *The Journals of Søren Kierkegaard*, cd. Alexander Dru (New York: Harper & Brothers, 1959), 245, quoted in Richard Foster, *Prayer: Finding the Heart's True Home* (San Francisco: Harper-SanFrancisco, 1992), 54.

3. Thomas Merton, *Thoughts in Solitude* (Boston: Shambhala, 1993), 47.

4. Macrina Wiederkehr, *A Tree Full of Angels: Seeing the Holy in the Ordinary* (San Francisco: HarperSanFrancisco, 1988), 68.

5. Wiederkehr, *Tree Full of Angels,* 11.

6. Catherine Marshall, *Adventures in Prayer* (New York: Ballantine, 1975), 62.

7. Esther de Waal, *Living with Contradiction: An Introduction to Benedictine Spirituality* (San Francisco: Harper & Row, 1989), 93.

8. Dale Galloway, quoted in Alan E. Nelson, *Broken in the Right Place* (Nashville: Nelson, 1994), 88-89.

Chapter 16: Moving Forward

1. Vincent J. Donovan, *Christianity Rediscovered: An Epistle from the Masai* (England: SCM, 1982), 62-63, quoted in Roger Pooley and

Philip Seddon, eds., *The Lord of the Journey* (London: Collins, 1986), 118-19.

2. The Epistle to Diognetus, 9, quoted in Maxwell Staniforth, trans., *Early Christian Writings: The Apostolic Fathers* (New York: Penguin, 1968), 180-81; Pooley and Seddon, *The Lord of the Journey,* 281.

3. Thomas Kelly, *A Testament of Devotion* (New York: Harper & Row, 1941), 45.

4. John Cassian, *Conferences,* The Classics of Western Spirituality, trans. Colm Luibheid (New York: Paulist Press, 1985), 116.

5. Augustine, *Confessions,* trans. Henry Chadwick (Oxford: Oxford University Press, 1991), 201.

6. Harold L. Myra, *Living by God's Surprises* (Waco, TX: Word, 1988).

7. C. S. Lewis, *The Lion, the Witch and the Wardrobe* (New York: Macmillan, 1950), 75-76.

ABOUT THE AUTHOR

TIMOTHY JONES leads a campus ministry at Middle Tennessee State University and is an associate pastor at St. Paul's Episcopal Church in Murfreesboro, Tennessee. He travels widely, speaking and leading retreats. He is also the author of several noted books on the spiritual life, including *Awake My Soul, A Place for God, Nurturing a Child's Soul,* and the best-selling *Celebration of Angels.* With pollster George Gallup Jr., he coauthored *The Next American Spirituality.* He lives in the Nashville area with his wife and children.

For more information about Timothy Jones or to arrange speaking engagements and retreats, please write to:

Timothy Jones
PO Box 1222
Nolensville, TN 37135
Web address: www.theartofprayer.org